Through the Eyes of Betsy McCall

by

C. R. Perk

1663 LIBERTY DRIVE, SUITE 200
BLOOMINGTON, INDIANA 47403
(800) 839-8640
www.authorhouse.com

This book is a work of non-fiction. Names of people and places have been changed to protect their privacy.

© 2004 C. R. Perk
All Rights Reserved.

No part of this book may be reproduced, stored in a retrieval system, or transmitted by any means without the written permission of the author.

First published by AuthorHouse 08/09/04

ISBN: 1-4184-1334-8 (sc)

Printed in the United States of America
Bloomington, Indiana

This book is printed on acid-free paper.

Dedication

I would like to dedicate this book to the memory of Elsie Lee Rawls Mattes, and her widowed still living husband Harold Joseph Mattes. These are the real names of the self sacrificing couple that took on the added burden of three malnourished and emotionally challenged children; despite their own struggles to build a home and raise five children of their own.

Without their generous efforts and steadfast determination to create productive well adjusted people from my siblings and I, God Himself only knows where we would have all ended up in our lives. Without their diligent efforts this book would have never been written.

Where ever she is in God's Kingdom, it is a comfort for me to know in my heart that she will be there when I arrive, and it is my prayer that now in God's care that she and my mother have reconciled for all of eternity.

Prologue

May, 2002

I was sitting in the passenger seat of the Toyota Tacoma, watching the odometer reading as it crept to speeds in excess of eighty miles per hour. My husband, Roger was sleeping in the very cramped back seat, and my son of eighteen years was driving the truck. Seth was driving at this ridiculous rate of speed because as all youth in this country today, he was in a hurry.

We had all been in attendance at his 22 year old sister's college graduation in Tallahassee, Florida. We were now driving the six hours south toward both of our homes. Seth had spent two days in a very plush motor home with his father and grandparents. He was ready to get out from under their watchful eyes and hook up with his friends back home. Therefore, he asked if he could ride back with us. I had no objections in fact, I was strongly in favor of the additional time that this would allow me to spend with him, but his father and grandparents were not so eager to give him this freedom. Roger and I found it ridiculous that at the age of eighteen he was still so closely scrutinized, it was no wonder that he wanted to get away from them. I was also all too familiar with how stifling these people could be. I was totally in Seth's favor. In the end his wishes were granted, and he was on his way back home and driving our Toyota Tacoma.

At first I was nervous about Seth driving at these speeds. I was not overly confident of his skills behind the wheel since he had only had a license for about a year. But he was very proficient in his driving skills and I soon relaxed. I watched him without him even knowing that I was doing so. I could not get over how handsome he had become. No longer my little boy and showing distinct signs of manhood, he was now handling the truck as if he had been driving his entire life.

I settled in and relaxed, my mind fading back to a much earlier time when I was riding in another vehicle on this same stretch of Interstate at speeds in excess of eighty miles per hour.

Part 1

C. R. Perk

Through the Eyes of Betsy McCall

Chapter 1

May, 1987

I was sitting in the back seat of the four-door Audi, and the car was being driven by my brother in law, Sky. In the front passenger seat was a friend of Sky's named Luke. Sky was five years my junior, as well as his friend Luke. Sky had flown to Illinois to retrieve the 1980 Audi and the three of us had stopped in Nashville for a day of honky tonkin and drinking. This was something that Sky, Mack and I had done on several occasions when Sky had been living there and attending college. It seemed only appropriate that Sky should invite me along for the trip. It was a good time for all of us but the party was over now and it was back to reality.

"Why are you driving so fast?" I asked Sky.

"I don't want you to miss your flight," he responded.

We were in route to Tampa International Airport where I was to catch a flight back to Illinois. I did not think that I was in any danger of missing my flight, although I did not say as much. I just settled in for the ride, listening to the radio and chatting mindlessly with Luke.

We arrived at the airport with time to spare and yet Sky was still practically running to the terminal where I was to board the flight. We had barely time to check in when a short chubby middle-aged man approached me I had never seen before in my life.

"Are you Charletta Hunsdorfer?" he asked.

"Yes, I am." I replied

He then handed me a large bundle of legal documents, mumbled something about being appointed to deliver this document by the Sarasota County something or other and then walked away.

"Wait a minute," I said to the back of the stranger's head, "what is this?"

He made no response and continued to walk away. I looked at Sky for some type of explanation. Luke was nervously backing away.

"I had nothing to do with this," Sky said to me. "Why don't you just go into the lounge here and have a beer."

He almost shoved me into the lounge, escorting me by the arm. Then he and Luke quickly vanished in to the crowd.

I sat with the much needed beer, and smoking mindlessly. I opened the document and attempted to decipher what was for the most part Greek to me.
'In the county of Sarasota, in the State of Florida… Plaintiff states that he is a resident of Florida …the plaintiff further states that as a resident of Florida…'
What in the hell did Mack think he was doing? I've got to call home and find out what is going on. I was very confused and not really thinking rationally. I thought I knew what this was about, but because I didn't want to believe it I choose not to.
I phoned my best friend Susan who was in Illinois. "Susan," I said somewhat hysterically, "I need for you to go to the house and see if anyone is there. I change flights in Dayton and I will call you again from there."

As the plane made its way to Dayton, I recalled the events of the night before. We had all had more than enough to drink but I was not totally without conscious. After Sky went to bed, Luke came to the sofa where I was to sleep and attempted to seduce me. It was not a forceful attempt and he quietly left me when he was rejected, but I now wondered if this was part of the master plan.

When my flight landed in Dayton, my apprehension mounting, I phoned Susan again.
"The house is dark Charlie. Your car is there, Chelsea the dog is there, but no one else is there," she said.
"Shit! I can't believe this!" I said
My greatest fears now a reality I simply asked Susan, "Will you please pick me up at the airport, my flight arrives at 8:40."
Susan agreed to pick me up.

I sat in coach seated beside a man who became increasingly uncomfortable with my uncontrollable tears. Reality was creeping in and I could not stop the tears as my mind raced backwards in time. How could this have happened again my mind screamed, how could this happen twice in one lifetime? The stranger beside me nervously glanced at me and made a well-meaning comment, "Something very sad has happened to you." he said. It was really more of a question than a comment, to which I simply nodded my head. This was not something I was prepared to discuss with total strangers and idol chitchat was out of the question. Reality had hit without mercy now. I should never have boarded this flight. I should have walked to Sarasota if necessary, but I should not have left the state of Florida!

At long last my flight arrived in Champaign, Illinois. I disembarked from the aircraft and entered the terminal. Inside the terminal was a couple that were friends of Mack's and mine. It really would not have mattered who was there to meet me. Anyone that I knew, and felt safe with was going to release the same reaction. I towered over both of their short frames by a head and I don't know how the two of them managed to hold me in an upright position. Oblivious to the stares of curious on lookers, my pent up heartache, and gripping fear exploded when I saw their familiar faces. I wailed hysterically, as these two slight people caught my collapsing frame.
"He stole my babies! The Son of a Bitch stole my babies!"
"We know," Debbie responded as the two of them caught me when I fell into their arms. "He called us and told us what he had done. He asked us to meet you here when your flight came in."
"The Son of a Bitch stole my babies!" I wailed again. "I can't believe he would steal my babies!"
"Neither can we and we do not agree with what he has done," she softly stated, "Now come over here and sit down."
The two of them half dragged, half carried me to the seats in the terminal.

Chapter 2

The following day I awoke at the marital residence, which was not our home, but belonged to his parents. As Susan had stated the family dog was there, my car, and of course no children. Also there was the unsigned "Shared Parental Custody Agreement" that I'd had a local attorney draft before I left the state with Skyler.

To say that I was stupid for the foolish trust that I had placed in Sky is a ridiculous understatement. He was a traitor to me and he had lied about his involvement and his motives. He was the key component to this child abduction being accomplished successfully, and I had naively trusted him and his older brother, my husband, Mack.
"I would never take our kids away from you," Mack had promised me months before.
Yet that is exactly what he had just done! I had been advised by my mother not to go with Sky. My "toy friend", Jay had advised me not to go with Sky. Still I did not heed their warnings. I truly believed that I could trust these people despite the deteriorating marriage. In my wildest imagination, I never thought that Mack would be so careless with the children's emotional well being, especially after everything that we had already endured.

When I mentally recovered from the initial shock that he had actually stolen our children, I became filled with rage. Anger is far too weak of a word to describe my feelings at that time. After having lived a farce for so many years, it was easy for me to put on a strong front and appear brave and confident; and that is exactly what I made myself do. Once again I did not leave the privacy of my home without full make up and dress, and no one other than a select few actually saw the reality of my suffering.

I contacted the local attorney who had drafted the "Shared Parental Custody Agreement" and informed her of what had taken place. She and her husband had been social contacts with Mack and I, and our children had played together. She wisely declined my request that she act as my council advising me that this would create a conflict of interest. She did however refer me to another attorney from my hometown, which is a slightly larger town about twenty-five miles south of where the marriage had been lived.

The marriage had been lived in a small rural farm community in the heart of Amish country in central Illinois. This community was centrally located amidst three fairly large towns, thus the residents could go to other towns for movies, shopping, and as in my case, an indifferent attorney.

I started looking for financial help from family and friends, but this was an act of futility.

There was no support either financially or emotionally. My family had turned their backs to me. I was twenty-nine years old; I had no formal education, no work history, no money, and certainly no knowledge of the judicial systems in either Illinois or Florida. I felt extremely overwhelmed by all of this, but I was not yet beaten.

Mack and I owned a duplex in town where we had lived before we moved to his parent's house in the country. We had leased out both units but I illegally evicted the tenant that was occupying the side that we had previously lived in. I now know that the action to evict a tenant without provocation and without an appropriate amount of notice so that the tenant can make other arrangements is totally illegal. I know that now, but I did not then. Amazingly the tenant complied.

In the days that I had to wait for the tenant to move out of the duplex, I ransacked the home of my husband's parents. I took ceiling fans that Mack and I had hung, leaving bare wires hanging from the ceiling and uncapped. Even as angry as I was I would not have left a fire hazard if I had known the first thing about electricity and live wires. I took everything that had been marital property, but nothing that belonged to his parents that had been left for our comfort. In the wake of moving out of the marital residence, I made a point of cleaning nothing, which is very much unlike me. I did not really deliberately destroy anything, but neither did I do anything to make the inevitable clean up easy. I left the residual matter that always exists when a family moves out of a dwelling. I did this willfully and with malice as a signature statement. The message; 'Kiss my ass!'

After the tenant had left the duplex, I moved all of my personal effects, my dog Chelsea, and myself into the unit. Jay was not invited but he made every effort to get his possessions in the door. He would carry his clothes in; I laundered them and carried them back out. He did not understand that this was not my backwards little community, it was Mack's and I was already not very popular. Having Jay around all the time only exacerbated the community's judgment of me. I knew this and I also knew that his junky old car parked in front of my house did nothing to assist me in my quest to get my children back.

My Illinois attorney was a very ambitious man. I think he saw a great deal of notoriety and publicity as a result of this custody battle. When I entered his very impressive office I met a tall slender man in his early thirties. He had a nervous tendency to adjust his neck- tie all the time and his nails were bitten down to small stubs on the ends of his fingers. Yet despite his nervous tendencies I had a good deal of faith in his abilities to advise me on my rights and to protect my interests. The small town local attorney had given me good advice.

When I entered his office I had mustered all the confidence I could find within myself. I wore a red tank top with a black skirt, a red belt around the waist and a pair of red flat shoes. I shook the hand of David Ebers, and he motioned for me to sit.

I informed him that Mack had stolen my children and ran to Florida with them. I showed him the papers that I had been served, the now worthless Shared Parental Custody Agreement and briefly filled him in on my case.
"I can only begin proceedings for a divorce motion," he said. "He has already made a motion for the custody hearings to be held in Florida. That complicates the situation but we can further complicate matters by locking him into the Illinois judicial system."
"So I have to go back to Florida?" I asked incredulously.
"Well not exactly, at least not right now," He said.
"Our first move is to make him come back to Illinois for an alimony hearing," he said "So I will get a motion going to lock him into our court system, and then will we have to find an attorney for you in Florida.

"Two attorneys, wonderful," I said knowing full well that I had no way of paying these high dollar legal fees.

"They have already locked you into an evidentiary hearing to determine if the custody battles should be held in the Illinois judicial system, or the Florida judicial system," he explained to me.

"I can't believe that he can get away with this," I said, "Isn't it against the law for him to just remove the children from the marital state?" I asked

"No," he replied, "he has the same rights that you have and he can take his children where ever he wants to, but he has to prove to the Florida courts that there is just cause for your case to be heard under their jurisdiction and not that of the marital state."

This was becoming increasingly more complicated and my inner strengths were wavering, but I did not want Mr. Ebers to know this. I had to be a pillar of strength, because I knew that Mack would use my emotional history in court. I had to be strong; I had to show them all that I was not unstable and that I was capable and fit as a parent. Mack knew that I was a very fit parent, more so than most, but I now realized that he would stop at nothing to discredit me.

"So how do I find an attorney in Florida?" I asked.

He swiftly spun his huge office chair around and grabbed a thick book from the many that aligned the shelves behind him. He began thumbing through the pages until he came to a section that seemed to satisfy his search. He ran his finger down the page until he came upon more information and then he picked up the telephone on the edge of his desk and dialed a phone number. He had a brief conversation with someone on the extension about my case, hung up the phone and announced that I had an attorney in Florida.

"His name," he said, "is Joe Johnson"

"Ok," he said, as he leaned back in his massive chair and once again adjusted his tie, "this is what I want you to do. Do not make the mortgage payment on the duplex; get everything of value and everything that you want from the marital residence; I want you to call your children every day, and for Gods sake don't come to court dressed as you are now!"

This final statement took me back a little. Did he think that I was a total moron? Perhaps, but I really didn't care. He was on my payroll not the

other way around. I informed him that I had already taken every thing that I wanted from the marital residence.
He then asked, "Are there any other assets between Mack and you?"
"There is only the stuff that is in our business office." I replied.
"Get it!" he said, "we want every asset we can get into your possession."

So again we shook hands, I thanked him for his time and I left his office feeling a little more confident that I did when I had arrived. Now I was on a mission. Somehow I had to get inside the small business office that was owned by Mack's father, but used by us in Mack's small failing commodities business. It's ironic that I had no key to a jointly owned business, but I did not. In hindsight I realize that this is indicative of the position that women hold in the minds of Mack and his family. Now faced with the dilemma of obtaining a key, I contacted Mack's father's secretary whom I knew would have a key.
"Janice," I said, "I did not take any of the furniture from the farm and I need the old brown sofa from the office, so I can use it for the apartment. Can I borrow the key to get into the office?" Janice, who was a devoted Hundsorfer family friend, gave me the key without any concern that I would do more than take the old brown sofa. I liked Janice and I hated doing this to her, but this was my war, not hers. She was just a casualty.

Jay and I entered the office and had a field day. We took a dedicated computer system that was linked to the Chicago Board of Trade, a very expensive telephone system including the control box that we took from the wall, the big screen television that was used to display each day's trading activities; and even the old brown sofa.

I returned the key to Janice as innocently as I had borrowed it, took my loot home and locked it up just as my wise attorney had advised me to do. This move staggered Mack, and his family. Suddenly they all realized that they were not dealing with the wimp that they had molded me into over the past ten years. My greatest regret in this bold move was Janice who came to my door to express her disappointment in me and to say that she had trusted me to take only the sofa.
"I had trusted Mack not to take my children." I responded.

Mr. Ebers contacted me soon after this to inform me that the jurisdictional hearing would be on Tuesday of the following week and I could listen to the hearing if I telephoned at the time of the hearing. Mr. Joe Johnson, whom I had briefly spoken to, was to appear on my behalf. So on the date of the hearing I telephoned.
"Mrs. Hunsdorfer, can you hear us?" I heard the Judge ask.
"Yes, I can hear you," I replied
"Councils you may proceed," the Judge said

Mack's attorneys did most of the talking, advising the Judge that this hearing was a jurisdictional hearing. He advised the Courts that Mack had filed for custody in the State of Florida and was claiming to be a resident of Florida. How Mack got away with the farce that he was a resident of Florida in a matter of two days I have never understood, but apparently the courts accepted it as a fact.

Mr. Joe Johnson responded in my defense that I was the mother of the children and still residing in the State of Illinois. He further informed the courts that I had petitioned for disillusion in the state of Illinois, and then he went on to tell the Court that he was not prepared for this hearing and asked for a continuance.

"So what we have here is a race to the court house?" the Judge asked sarcastically.
"Yes your Honor." Mack's council responded.

The Judge called for a continuance.
I hung up the phone and I knew that I was in over my head. My Florida attorney was no David Ebers, and he had no more interest in helping me get my children back than Mack had of returning them. I suspected that the Hunsorfers and their son in law attorney had already gotten to Mr. Joe Johnson and lined his wallet with currency.

Chapter 3

After taking most everything of value, knowing full well what money meant to these people, and having taken possession of the duplex. I had everything that he valued and he had everything that I valued, but I would have been open to a trade at any time. No such offers were made.

The realization that my Florida attorney was inept was a terrible blow. I had asked him prior to this hearing if he wanted school records, proof of activity involvement, anything that I could find that would substantiate the children's well being was in their home state with their mother. That was a marvelous idea Joe Johnson thought, but not one that he ever utilized. As diligently as I had tried to create an illusion that I was the pillar of strength, I was only a very small rumble away from a total collapse, and the collapse came soon after the first hearing.

Jay and I were still using the golf privileges at the local country club where Mack and I had played for years. The cart was there and the dues were paid, there was nothing anyone could do to stop us. One afternoon when we were playing, I was paged from the course for an emergency phone call. I returned to the clubhouse to take the call, my apprehension mounting.
"Hello," I said without a clue as to who might be on the end of the line.
It was Susan, "Charlie" she said with real pain and anxiety in her voice, "the maintenance man at the retirement home behind the duplex called me and said that Chelsea is dead."
"Is that all? I asked feeling greatly relieved. "There is no way." I flatly stated. I had been so concerned that the call involved my children that the dog was of little consequence and quite frankly I did not believe it,
"Susan, have you been to the house to check on her," I asked.
"No," she responded, "He called me at work. I just called you to tell you what he told me."
"Susan that dog was fine when I left her chained this morning to the clothes line. She could move the entire length of the line and she had plenty of fresh water. There was absolutely nothing wrong with her when I left this morning." I said defiantly. I was so convinced that this was a very bad

joke that someone was playing on me that I returned to the golf course and finished my round of golf.

However, when Jay and I returned to the duplex, there lying in the back yard was a very dead AKC registered Boxer. Chelsea was really dead!

My relief was short lived and I was broken hearted. I could not fathom what had happened to her. The night before I had bathed her and put meatloaf dripping on her dog food. She had been perfectly fine!

If I'd had any money I would have had an autopsy performed to confirm what I already knew, that my dog had been poisoned, but I did not. Susan's husband buried her in the back yard of the duplex, while Susan and I cried our hearts out.

"How am I going to tell the kids that Chelsea is dead? I asked Susan through my tears.

Susan had no words of wisdom for me because there were none. I had a pretty good idea which of my neighbors had murdered my dog, and this act of cruelty only served to confirm that my popularity was not in good standing.

After the murder of my family pet and the disastrous first hearing, I was brought to the point of total devastation.

I laid on the sofa in the duplex and studied the photographs on the wall of my two beautiful children. I was hurt on a level that I had never known before and I longed for death. I refused food, I did not shower, I did not brush my hair or my teeth, I did not dress and I did not leave the safety of the duplex. I laid on the sofa that I had taken from the office, crying and contemplating suicide. It was not the first time that I had considered something so rash, although previously I had hoped for Mack's death, not my own.

"I should have let him drown that day," I said to no one but myself.

Mack had little swimming skills and he once jumped off of a moving boat while under the influence of alcohol. The boat had been shut off but was quickly moving away from him. At first he yelled, "Hey, don't leave me," with humor in his voice. Then he suddenly began to panic realizing that this was not funny. The boat was drifting further away from him and he did not

have the skill to swim to us. I knew this, and I hesitated to throw him a line and floatation.
"Charlie," he had cried out to me, truly in a panic, "help me!"
I was mortified by the realization that I had hesitated, even for a second. I quickly threw him floatation and a line and I pulled him safely back to the boat. I had not let him drown that day, although right now I wished that I had.

Once again I recalled the evening when he and I had discussed what I would do if anyone ever tried to take my children from me.
"I will walk to where they are if I have to." I had said with great confidence.
"I would never take the children from you." He had said, and tragically I believed him. What a bunch of hypocrites these bible thumping Mennonites were. They had their false images to keep up but they were no more honest and God fearing than the rest of world. They march off to church each Sunday for fellowship and appearances, but come Monday morning they are as ruthless and dishonest as the rest of us. Mack and his family were no exception to this. In fact they were the epitome of it. I had trusted Mack to keep his word and I had trusted Sky. I was hurt by these betrayals but the anger was paramount.

Through episodic sleep I had the same reoccurring dream.
Mack was tied to a chair, jerking his head from side to side trying to see what I was doing. The room was full of marble pillars as if we were in a palace. I then walked up to him and pointed a gun between his eyes. My soul was utterly consumed with delight as I witnessed the fear that he displayed in his eyes. I then walked behind him and then to his side and put the gun against his temple.
"Goodbye Mack," I said.
"Charlie don't do this, please don't do this!" He cried as he thrashed his head from side to side in an effort to see what I was doing.
I slowly pulled the trigger; click. The chamber was empty.
I awakened somewhat frustrated each time this dream occurred. I recognized that I obviously did not have the disposition for murder, the palace setting was indicative of their wealth, and I was consumed by anger and the desire to control him as he had done to me for so many years.

These were very turbulent days for me emotionally. There were no highs; only lows and the lows were getting dangerously low. As much as I longed for death to come and stop the pain I knew that I could not kill myself. There was no way that I could abandon my children and Mack knew this too. I believed that he took the children because he thought I would reconcile with him for the love of my children. While my heart ached for the absence of my children, it also softly rejoiced with its newly found freedom. Even for the love of my children, I could not go back.

As my mind once again slid backwards in time, I had to wonder how God could have allowed such a tragedy to occur twice in twenty- nine years.

C. R. Perk

Through the Eyes of Betsy McCall

Part 2

C. R. Perk

Chapter 4

Spring 1963:
The train lumbered through the Rocky Mountains and across the great plains of North America, ever so slowly approaching our destination in central Illinois.
"We are going to visit the sweetest woman in the whole world," my Sister had said to me.
She was fifteen years old, and ten years my senior. Also present for this journey was my brother who was nine years older than me and both were my unyielding heroes. The trip was basically uneventful except for the military personnel that my sister kept flirting with, and the great fear that I harbored that one or both of them would not get back on the train when it stopped along the way. The whistle sounded at every stop announcing that the train was about to depart and I sat on the train in horror because one of them had not yet come back.

The journey took a total of three days and two nights, an eternity to a five year old. At long last we arrived in the small rural town of Mattoon, Illinois, and there to greet us was the sweetest woman in the world, our Aunt Elise. She was the sister of my mother whom we had left behind in southern California. The sweetest woman in the world was a tall blonde woman with a thin build, green eyes and very erect posture. She gave us each a hug and shuttled us off to her car. The three of us rode with her to the three-bedroom single story home where she lived with her husband and five children.

We entered the house and there were the five children and Aunt Elise's kind husband, Uncle Howard. The five children's ages ranged from two to nine and I found them to be overwhelming. This was their turf, not mine and they were clearly very comfortable with the arrival of three new visitors. They were in fact rather excited about our intrusion in to their home. I was intimidated. Their children were well adjusted and accustom to sharing the spot light. I had always been the center of attention and I did not have to share with anyone, <u>ever.</u>

The preliminary introductions were made, "This is Ellie, Boyd and Charletta Raye," Aunt Elise told her children. Then she told us the names of her five children starting with the youngest. "This is Donna, she is two, this is Royce, he is four, this Mitch and he is seven, this is Daniel and she is eight, and this is Clarice, she is nine." With the introductions being complete, Aunt Elise went into full sing and began making demands of us immediately.

The first thing that the sweet Aunt Elise did was to take our small box of personal belongings away.

"I want you all in the tub and showers immediately!" she had stated very sternly.

"You first," she stated pointing to my sister.

Ellie my sister complied as she was told and went to the shower. I began to follow her to the bathroom so that I would not be separated from her.

"Where do you think you are going?" asked Aunt Elise. "Ellie doesn't need your help in the shower."

"It's alright," said Ellie. "She can come with me."

"No she cannot," said Aunt Elise, and I was ordered away from the bathroom.

In tears I coward from the very demanding aunt and coddled to my brother, Boyd in Ellie's absence.

When Ellie had finished her shower, Aunt Elise entered the bathroom with her. After a short time she came back out and then ordered Boyd to the shower.

Boyd complied and entered the bathroom for his shower and I felt greatly relieved that I could be reinstated to Ellie's side.

When Boyd had finished his shower it was my turn, and at least Ellie was allowed to go in to the bathroom with me while I took a bath.

We were all given clean clothes to wear that did not belong to us, and then to my horror all of our clothes were taken to the barrel in the back yard where they were burned.

Although not the same night that we arrived but soon thereafter I was subjected to the horrible dinner hour where the main course on the menu was beef liver.

"Just tell her that it is red chicken and she'll eat it," Ellie had said to the family. "She likes red chicken, but she hates liver."

We all sat at the table and everyone bowed their heads.

"Bless us O Lord and these thy gifts which we are about to receive, in thy bounty through Christ Our Lord, Amen," the family of seven all said in unison.

I had bowed my head like everyone else had done, but I had never heard such a mumbo jumbo bunch of words that meant nothing to me.

After grace was said, the plates were served and we all prepared to eat the meal before us.

"It's liver, it's liver and you have to eat it!" Danielle, their eight year old had chided me with absolute glee. Danielle had immediately set herself up as my rival and everything that she could do to torment me she seemed to delight in.

I was mortified! Tears began to stream down my cheeks and I wailed that I did not like liver. Ellie's effort had failed and now aware of what was before me, I was determined not to eat it. No one ever made me eat what I did not want!

Aunt Elise did not see things the same way that I did.

"In this house you will eat what is prepared, and you will clean your plate. Do you understand me?" asked Aunt Elise.

I searched the faces around me and looked to Ellie and Boyd for support. They only began to eat and looked at the food in front of them.

Through my tears I sat and picked at my plate for a very long time.

"I don't like it." I persisted in my misery.

"You will sit here until you eat it." Said Aunt Elise.

"Ellie said that you were nice, but you're not! You're mean!" I wailed defiantly at Aunt Elise, through my tears.

"Mean or not, you are in my house and while you are in my house you will eat what is prepared for you. Do you understand?" Asked Aunt Elise.

"My mommy doesn't make me eat things that I don't like." I wailed. "I want to go home!" I shouted at her through my tears.

"Well you are here now, and you will eat what is on your plate." Announced Aunt Elise without diplomacy, "and you will sit here until you do." She reiterated.

Sit there I did with a small portion of liver in front of me, for many hours. How many is hard to say. At this early stage of the "visit' I may have actually out lasted her demands and defied her wishes that I clean my plate. I was much more experienced at getting my way, than Aunt Elise was at being challenged.

The next tragedy that occurred involved a bride doll that I had coddled for as long as I could remember. She was made in 1948 and her name was Betsy McCall. Betsy had blue eyes that moved loosely in the eye sockets according to the angle of the head, she had a long white gown, auburn hair, and her head and limbs were held together by a large rubber band. Royce, one of their five children who was not yet five, took Betsy and broke the rubber band that held her limbs to her torso.

"He broke my doll!" I screamed at the top of my lungs, again tears streaming down my face. Betsy was now six pieces of rubber lying in my lap and I was devastated. This was the ultimate blow and I could stand no more, "I want my mommy!" I wailed.
The very kind Uncle Howard did the obvious and re-rubber banded Betsy back together for me. This greatly helped to relieve the immediate tragedy that had just occurred, but I still wanted my mommy! The days came and went, still the visit did not end, and my mommy never came and got me.

During that first summer that I was thrown into this 'visit', I learned that Aunt Elise and Uncle Howard owned a lot on the local lake. It was nothing but a lot of land with a boat slip, and a wooden seawall. One Saturday the five children got all excited about the days plans of going to the lake and have a cook out. I had never been to a lake so I was rather excited too. Uncle Howard was going to take his boat down on a trailer, take a grill and we would all have a lovely time.
When we arrived at the lake everything appeared to be all right, although I was leery of getting into the water. After some coercion Ellie and Boyd convinced me that I had nothing to fear and that I should go into the lake. I timidly entered the lake and immediately got back out.
"Its muddy on the bottom and I can't see anything," I said
All of the other children laughed at my fears.
"You're stupid," they said. "Get in, nothing is going to hurt you."
"I don't like it," I said defiantly, and nothing was going to get me back into that muck.
A day at the lake was way overrated in my estimation. This was not fun!

Later that same day it was discussed that we would have to get me enrolled in school for the following school year.
"I don't want to go to school," I said "I want to go home to my mommy."
"No," Ellie said, "You need to go to school where you can learn to read and write, and do math problems and someday algebra and geometry."
Immediately I began to cry again, because I did not even know what algebra and geometry were, but I was certain I was afraid of them. I could not do these hard things.
The older three of the five began to tease me because I was crying.
"I've already been to school," I defended myself.
"When did you go to school?" Danielle asked me.
"In California with my mommy," I yelled back at her.
It had actually been a childcare facility, but I had been told it was school so that I was a big girl like Ellie and Boyd.
"Then you're stupid," she said. "You flunked kindergarten and now you have to repeat it."
The tears continued, I wanted my mommy more than ever, but the real tragedy is that I believed her. If I had already flunked kindergarten then I must be stupid.

I really did not like this visit very much and I did keep asking when we were going home.
No one ever once satisfied that question with an answer. These people were mean to me and they made fun of me. Aunt Elise was not sweet and Uncle Howard was going to eat me. Royce had broken my doll and Danielle said I was stupid. I grew increasingly more depressed and more determined than ever to return to my mommy.

The single story home with the three bedrooms had a converted garage that was made into a toy room. I did like the toy room. The toy room was full of neat things to sit on and ride like rocking horses and lots of crayons and chalk and chalk boards. It was really a family room with a sewing machine, television (for a limited amount of time), furnishings to be destroyed by children and the toys. There was a sliding door that exited to the back patio, and when the floor of the toy room was swept, the dirt and debris were simply swept out the back door. As a result of sweeping matter out the back sliding door, I experienced a rather unusual accident.

I was riding a small bicycle with training wheels on the back yard patio when the bike started to tip as I entered the grass. I put my feet down to catch myself before it toppled over and I experienced an agonizing pain in my left foot. I immediately began to cry as I so often did in those days and wobbled into the house.
Aunt Elise inspected my foot and found no evidence of any injury with the exception of a very small droplet of blood on the bottom of my foot. I continued to cry and Uncle Howard inspected my foot with the same findings. There was no evidence of any damage to my foot.
"You are fine, now go play," I was instructed.
"She cries all the time!" my Aunt Elise declared. "There is nothing wrong with her foot."
So off I went as I was instructed to do, but I did so with my foot cocked so that I walked on its side.

I was also loosing my first two teeth on the bottom and my new permanent teeth were nearly in behind them. Uncle Howard tried numerous times to get me to let him into my mouth with a set of pliers to extract these two teeth, but I would not have any part of it.
He was a kind man, but he would put ketchup on my arm and tell me that he liked to eat little girls, and then he would lick it off. This man had the biggest teeth that I had ever seen and I was certain that he had the capability of devouring me in a single bite. It scared the living hell out of me and when I cried from this fear, he would further humiliate me by catching my tears with a spoon.

After walking on the side of my foot for two weeks, both my aunt and uncle conceded that even I could not pretend to have an injury for this length of time. I was an unhappy child, and I cried an inordinate amount of the time, but something had to be wrong with that foot. So I was finally taken in for x-rays that revealed a foreign body wedged through the bone in my left foot.

Soon thereafter I had surgery and the rusty needle that went into my foot with such a clean entry was removed from the bone. When I awoke from surgery, I found my left foot in a cast, but the most annoying thing was the lumpy sensation in the front of my mouth on the bottom. Someone had removed my baby teeth!

Then suddenly Aunt Elise became very nice to me. She came to see me everyday while I was in the hospital and she brought me toys. I learned the alphabet while I laid in that hospital bed, and she brought me M & M's, books, paper dolls and I started to think that maybe she wasn't so mean after all.

Those promising thoughts were short lived however. I soon learned that the surgery had been the easy part. The nurses brought me cherry flavored medicines that I swallowed without reservation, but after the first of what was to be a series of Tetanus shots, I became distraught all over again. No child likes a vaccination of any sort, but this was excessive. I felt like a pincushion and when the nurses entered the room with a syringe I reacted violently. I physically attempted to fight them off. If there was anyway to avoid another injection, I was going to find it. I physically resisted the nurses fighting their every effort to overcome me and I shouted at them, "No, no, no!" as I flung my arms and legs around the bed and into the air.

The nurses were overwhelmed by my noncompliance as a patient and they cornered Aunt Elise when she came in to see me. They told her of my hysterical behavior.
"You will stop this nonsense when the nurses come in to administer your shots young lady, and I don't want to hear of anymore fits. If I hear that you fight the nurses again, I will beat your butt. Do you hear me?" asked Aunt Elise.
One would think that a spanking would be far preferable to a shot, but the wrath of Aunt Elise carried much weight.
I nodded my head solemnly, because I had now learned to fear her. There would be no more tantrums when the nurses came to give me my shots. I would have to obey my aunt for now, but I knew that my mommy was going to come get me soon.

C. R. Perk

The recovery from the freak accident and surgery should have been a breeze, but the injection sight became infected and I was required to soak my foot several times a day and my activities were restricted because I had to keep the dressings dry.

Chapter 5

This visit that had so traumatized me at the tender of age five was never really a visit and no one ever telling me that truth was the single greatest mistake of those adults who should have been more responsible with my emotional well being.

My mother was an incurable alcoholic and she was far less interested in providing for me, than finding her next drink. Consequently, I had no discipline and the responsibility of caring for my fundamental needs had come to rest on Ellie and Boyd's shoulders. They were fourteen and fifteen year old children trying to provide for the needs of a five-year-old child.

Our furniture and car had been repossessed; there was no food in our home and no mother present to care for us. Ellie and Boyd did their best to provide for our most fundamental needs, but they were supposedly in school and doing what they deemed necessary. I was home alone once and very hungry. I went to the barren refrigerator to find something to eat and finding nothing else, I ate raw bacon. On many other occasions, Ellie mixed flour and water together creating make believe biscuits. She baked this concoction and we ate it because it filled our stomachs.

Eventually when our mother had lost everything she had to lose, she moved us to a house in the country with her boyfriend who was many years her junior. Her boyfriend was still living at home with his parents and his mentally challenged brother.

Ellie and Boyd had been living their own private hells, each having experienced some type of sexual abuse in their young lives, the details of which are not my experiences to share. Miraculously I did not befall the same fate. Ellie in defiance kept running away from home. Our mother would eventually dry out and notice her absence and we would all go search for her and bring her back. Boyd was not so rebellious; he was content to try to survive this nightmare. Ellie would tell our mother over and over that she wanted to go live with her Aunt Elise. Our mother who had grown weary of chasing down a rebellious teenager finally conceded.

She and Ellie telephoned Aunt Elise and asked if Ellie could come live with her.
"Ellie," said Aunt Elise, "you understand that if you come live at my house, you will not run away and you will live by my rules?"
"Oh yes," cried Ellie.
Ellie had memories of Aunt Elise when she was a much smaller child and those memories were full of a kind and loving woman.
"Alright, I'll wire the money for you to come out here on the train." Said Aunt Elise, and Ellie was on her way to what she had come to perceive as her personal paradise.

When it came time for Ellie to travel north to our great aunt's home who was to help her get on the train, our mother was on one her binges. Ellie prepared to leave and Boyd said he wasn't staying! Between the two of them it was decided that they would both go and they sure as hell were not leaving me.

I don't even know how we all three got to our great aunts home, but I know that when we arrived, the great aunt telephoned Aunt Elise.
"Elise," she said, "it isn't just Ellie. They're all three here!"
Without hesitation Elise responded, "I'll send a wire for all their fares."
She did just that, and soon there after the train ride and the visit began.

When we arrived we were all three filthy, severely malnourished and our clothes were tattered rags. Boyd's face and back were pitted and covered with acne. Ellie and Boyd were both inspected for mites or obvious signs of sexually transmitted deceases following their showers and I'm sure my head was checked for lice and all of our bowel movements checked for parasites. It was due to malnutrition that my foot had become so infected following the surgery.

Aunt Elise really wasn't a tyrannical bitch as I had perceived her to be and Uncle Howard wasn't really going to eat me. She was not only a very good woman, but her intentions were noble and unquestionably self-sacrificing. She and Uncle Howard were saints. Aunt Elise had taken charge of a desperate situation and Uncle Howard was attempting to play with me. What couple with a family of seven including themselves would take on three more mouths to feed? Not only three additional mouths to feed, but also physically and emotionally emaciated children whom God himself only knew, what emotional baggage would come with them.

There was talk amongst Aunt Elise's family that they should split us up and her parents and other siblings should help to bear the burden in raising us. Aunt Elise was adamant on this subject; we would not be separated, and we were not.

At the age of five, I saw none of this. Aunt Elise was not my mother, and she never would be. My loyalty to my mother was far too strong for me to ever accept Aunt Elise as a surrogate parent and one day I knew that my real mother was coming to get me. This was after all only a 'visit'.

Chapter 6

The year slowly passed and my mother did not come to save me. There was not a card or even a telephone call, but in these formidable years my faith in her did not waiver. I continued to hold steadfast to the belief that she was coming. I had dreams of her coming to the front door and demanding my return to her loving care. Those fantasies lasted for many years.

Soon after our arrival, all ten of us moved into the dream home that Aunt Elise and Uncle Howard had been building. This was a five bed room, three bath, two-story home, with a full basement. When the plans were drawn up for this home, there were no plans for three additional people, but in the long run this big house turned out to be an enormous blessing.

I was slowly developing survival techniques that I did not recognize nor would I have understood them if I did recognize them. I still clung to Ellie and Boyd for emotional support, and this infuriated Aunt Elise.
"You and Boyd have got to stop parenting her," she had said to Ellie. "She will not accept me as her mother if you don't."

After that Ellie would not let me leave my bedroom where I shared a bed with their youngest child Donna, and slip into the safety of her bed. She told me that Aunt Elise did not approve and that I should not come to her room any more. It seemed to me that no matter what I did Aunt Elise did not approve and her entire motivation in this life was to make me unhappy. I did not understand why she was so mean and always taking something away that was important to me.

She did not understand that I would never accept her as my mother. My mother was alive and well and she was coming to save me. I held this faith in my heart everyday that Aunt Elise tried to be a good surrogate mother to me. Neither she nor I understood the psychological dynamics of how impossible it would have been for me to release those deep seeded feelings of loyalty to my mother, and I never understood that everything that she was trying to do was in my best interests.

"Why can't she just be happy?" Aunt Elise would ask Uncle Howard. Kind Uncle Howard had a better understanding of what tormented me so, but he was also reluctant to criticize the efforts of his well-meaning wife.

Aunt Elise had a strong stance against nicknames and she named all five of her children with names that could not be shortened or manipulated. Consequently, while everyone else in my world would call me Charlie, Aunt Elise refused and always referred to me as Charletta Raye. She always used both my first and middle name when she addressed me.
"Charletta Raye, pick up your room; Charletta Raye, brush your teeth, Charletta Raye do your homework…" and I grew to despise the sound of my own name. I developed a negative emotional reaction to the sound of my own name because it seemed that any time I heard my given name I was being corrected for something. Even Uncle Howard used my friendlier nickname of Charlie; my teachers honored my wishes that I be called Charlie, but not Aunt Elise. Each time I heard her say, "Charletta Raye," the hair stood up on the back of neck and I waited for the ax to fall.

I was nine years old when Ellie announced that she was getting married to a man in the army whom she had only dated for a short time while he was home on leave. Aunt Elise was mortified.
"You don't even know this man," she had argued. "And you are not going to marry him!"
"Oh, yes I am," said Ellie.
The argument continued, but there really wasn't anything that Aunt Elise could do to stop her. Ellie was legally an adult.
Aunt Elise said that Ellie's fiancé had contracted gonorrhea while overseas in Germany.
How she obtained this information is still a mystery to me, but a sexually transmitted decease is one those taboos that Aunt Elise felt was beneath our family. This man was not a suitable candidate for Ellie and she would not stand for this marriage.
Aunt Elise almost always got her way, but not this time.
Ellie and her soldier were united in matrimony without either the consent or presence of Aunt Elise and Uncle Howard.

This most strongly affected me when Ellie and her soldier packed up and moved to the army base in Colorado Springs, Colorado. I actually liked her new husband but I did not like him taking my life support system away. Still, I was not totally devastated by this although once again I felt that I had been abandoned. I still had Boyd, at least for now.

Then one year later, the ultimate tragedy struck! Boyd at the tender age of nineteen enlisted in the army!
"Why?" I wailed my question to Aunt Elise, "Why is he signing up to go to war?"
The Vietnam War was in full swing and my precious brother was signing up to go!
This had been one of my greatest fears from a very early time in my life. Even before being taken from my mother I still recalled the military troops marching in the processional for John F. Kennedy's funeral. At the age of four I knew that these men in uniforms were soldiers and that they had to fight wars. I probably drew this conclusion as a result of the media coverage of the Cuban Missile Crisis. I lived my early childhood in fear that one day Boyd would have to become a soldier, and that is exactly what was happening now.
My heart was frozen in fear, this time not for myself, but for Boyd. I could not control my anguish and tears of fear streamed down my face.
Aunt Elise was compassionate but stern when she said to me, "If he doesn't enlist, then he will just be drafted," she said.
"What is drafted?" I asked through my tears.
"That is when the government calls young men to the military services to defend our country and they have to go." She replied,
I was not hysterical, but I was devastated emotionally. I would now be left alone without either of my siblings to survive the wrath of Aunt Elise, but even worse was the fear that Boyd would not survive the combat of this war.

A special Mass was held for Boyd at our catholic church and I prayed as I had never prayed before. 'Please God don't let Boyd get killed in this war. Please God I prayed' over and over again. Then Boyd was gone.
He did not of course go to Vietnam immediately but to basic training in Missouri. I really didn't care where he had gone except that he was in the

war. We went to visit him once and then at the end of basic training he was to come home for a brief visit.

I was sitting in music class at school and Royce was in class with me because we joined classrooms for music. Royce whispered to me that Boyd was coming home today.
"Boyd is coming home?" I exclaimed too loudly for a classroom setting. The teacher looked at me sternly for the disruption but she said nothing.
I could hardly sit through the remainder of the school day. Boyd was coming home!
He had only been gone for six agonizing weeks, but he was coming home. I had no idea yet how long he would inevitably be removed from my life.

That night I sat on top of my bed and peered out the bedroom window with anticipation that every car that came down the long rural road toward our house was the one that Boyd was driving. How many hours I sat and watched for his car is hard to say, but I know that fatigue eventually overcame me and I had no choice but to succumb to slumber. Even more to my dismay, is that he had still not arrived when I awakened in the morning.

Eventually the skinny, pimply- faced nineteen year old did arrive and after a brief visit, he was gone again. This time he was not going to Missouri, but someplace on the other side of the world called Vietnam.

In our family room was a four-foot by six-foot map of Vietnam and Boyd's location in this far off land was pin pointed by pushpins. When he was moved, the pins were moved.
Aunt Elise bought special American treats and provisions for him and they were shipped to where ever he was. We no longer had a television set because Aunt Elise and Uncle Howard felt that is was detrimental to the growth and development of children, but during Boyd's internment in Vietnam we miraculously obtained a television for purposes of following the war. Cards and letters were sent to him and the entire family cherished the occasional letters that we received from him. The letters were written on air weight parchment and were hard to read due to Boyd's poor spelling and writing skills; but we made what we could from what he attempted to share with us about his life in this far away place.

These were difficult times for me, but they were equally difficult for Aunt Elise, our family, as well as the remainder of our great country. I did not understand the unpopularity of this war, and when I proudly declared to the school librarian that my brother was in this country; and I displayed a book on Vietnam; I had no idea why she responded with such irreverence if not almost contempt for what I had so proudly shared with her.

That year there were parent teacher conferences with respect to my academic performance or more truthfully that lack thereof. I was sat down by my teacher and advised that if I did not start to apply myself to my studies that I would not pass the fifth grade. Terrified of the embarrassment this would cause and the wrath of Aunt Elise, I applied enough to get through that grade level. On the final day of school I prayed to God that I would be advanced to the sixth grade, He must have heard my prayer.

Prayers are always answered, but not always when we ask for them, and one of my oldest prayers was finally answered during these very turbulent years. At long last I received a letter and pictures from my Mother. She had gotten married.
The pictures were of her before the ceremony and during. She was sharing with Aunt Elise and I how well she was doing, that she was back on her feet, and that she now wanted me back.

I was so confused. So many years of nothing and suddenly she wanted me to just leave this family. I was currently separated from Boyd and Ellie and my prayers had finally been answered, of course I wanted to go back to my mother.
Clarice, the oldest of the five children that I had been united with only five years before, came to me and said, "I don't want you to leave us, please don't go."
I was so confused because I suddenly realized that I had grown to love these people. So Aunt Elise wasn't on the top of my list, but I had shared a great deal with these children. Still my mother wanted me back and I had longed for this for so many years. I was so torn and it was very painful for me at this age, but I might not have bothered to agonize at all. Aunt Elise had obtained custody many years before, and I was not going anywhere.

Ellie's husband Joe was released from the military and they returned to central Illinois and set up house in the neighboring town of Charleston. They lived in a shack that belonged to his parents in a remote rural area. I loved going there to visit, and Aunt Elise once sent Donna, Royce and me to spend a week with them. Nothing significant occurred in that visit, I just loved the comfort of being in my big sisters home. Ellie was one of my life's loves and remains so to this day.

Boyd returned from Vietnam with all of his limbs in tact and I was greatly relieved that he had survived his time in that terrible war, but he wasn't a pimply face boy anymore.
He had become a man. He was taller and his physique was fuller, his hair was white from exposure to the blistering sun and his mouth was as foul as any I had ever heard.
"You pissed me off!" I heard Boyd say. He was only kidding around as he shot pool in our basement, but I was shocked to hear these things coming from his mouth.
He had learned to drink, smoke and cuss; and this was not at all like the Boyd that had left here two years earlier. To the total dismay of our God fearing housekeeper, Boyd hung Playboy centerfolds all over the walls in our family room. It really wasn't appropriate but no one was telling Boyd that he could not do this. He was home from Vietnam and his changed demeanor didn't offend even Aunt Elise. Perhaps she had a better understanding of what war does to young people than I could possibly have had.
In truth our family found his antics quite humorous until he got drunk and did not come home for several days. Aunt Elise was furious with him, but as always she forgave him.

Then suddenly Boyd brought a girl home with him. Her name was Colleen. She was very pretty with blonde hair and blue eyes; she was also pregnant and about to become Boyd's wife. So very soon after this first meeting with Colleen, our family was off to a neighboring town about thirty miles away for a church wedding in the spring of 1970. I had no problem adapting to Boyd's marriage to Colleen. I liked her and they made their home close to our home.

I had come to the realization that my mother was never coming for me, but I still longed for a reunion with her. I had come to accept that Aunt Elise, Uncle Howard, Clarice, Danielle, Mitch, Royce, Donna as well as Boyd and Ellie were my family. I never stopped planning the day that I would go to my mothers in California and spend my days on the sunny beach and live a life that I had only dreamed of, but for now I was resigned to the realization that I was a member of this household, like it or not. I had survived it this far and while I had not warmed to the stern Aunt Elise and still felt I could do nothing to please her, I simply endured.

"I don't understand her," she once said to Uncle Howard. "If I go upstairs, she goes down stairs. If am down stairs, she goes upstairs."
She did not understand that I did feel safe when she was around and this was my way of protecting myself from her critical and watchful eye.

Soon after Boyd and Colleen's marriage Aunt Elise had a large family gathering with her brother and sister in law present, Ellie, Joe, Boyd, Colleen and Aunt Elise's father and stepmother as well as myself and the remainder of our family. We were all sitting at a large table outdoors on our back yard patio eating, when Aunt Elise asked, "Charletta Raye have you told Ellie your news?"
Before I could say a word, Danielle piped up and shouted, "Charlie's a woman now!"
I was mortified! Was it really necessary for her to announce this private information to everyone at the table including my distant relatives? Was it really necessary for Aunt Elise to ask such a delicate question at this size of a gathering?
I jumped up from the table and ran around our large home to the front porch where I could endure my misery and embarrassment alone. I sat on the porch with tears in my eyes and to my astonishment; Joe came and sat beside me.

Joe marched to the beat of his own drum and was a bit of a misfit. He had little use for large family gatherings, even less use for the materialism of Aunt Elise and Uncle Howard, and I think he never forgave Aunt Elise for disapproving of him in the first place. Joe was what he was, but he had a big heart. He and I had bonded even before he married Ellie and here he was by my side in my tormented embarrassment.

"Don't let them get to you," he said. "This is just part of growing up."
"I know that, but they didn't have to tell everyone." I said through my tears.
"No, they didn't" he responded.
"You know what Danielle said when I told Aunt Elise that I had started my period; she said that I couldn't screw around now because I would get pregnant. I said ya right, and Aunt Elise glared at me like she thought that I was having sex."
"Elise has her own misguided delusions about sex and propriety," Joe said, "Try not to let her get to you."
He put his arm around me and we sat there for a while in silence, then he said, "Come on let's get back to the table."
I complied and later talked to Ellie privately about the coming of my menstrual cycle and all that I was about experience.
I was in full-blown puberty now and everything in my life was about to change.

Chapter 7

Prior to the onset of puberty, I had been a rather pitiful looking child. In addition to having deplorable posture, I wore horn-rimmed glasses and my mouth was too large for my face. The other children in the household made fun of my mouth all the time, especially Mitch, but even Boyd chimed into the hysterics at times. I hated my mouth and even worse was the fact that my baby teeth never fell out as other children's do. Uncle Howard was always in my mouth with a pair of pliers extracting baby teeth that had not fallen out naturally but had been pushed aside by the permanent teeth that were forging their way in. The baby teeth that Uncle Howard was extracting did not have root systems left on them, but the gum would not loosen and allow the tooth to fall out naturally. Uncle Howard misjudged only once when he extracted two teeth with the pliers and the roots were still intact. I sat there and allowed him to pull those teeth without anesthetic and I don't think even he could believe it when he had finished. He said he felt bad about it and to this day we share a chuckle when we talk about it.

At long last after having every baby tooth removed with pliers that could conceivably be removed, I finally had a full set of teeth, and they were perfectly aligned due to Uncle Howard's diligence to make room for the new permanent teeth. It seems barbaric but his intentions were honorable and he was trying to prevent future dental problems. However he did not succeed because I suddenly developed two new teeth in my upper gum on each side of my mouth and you could see these great white knolls in my gum when I smiled. Even Uncle Howard was not going to try to fix this problem, so off to the dentist I went and four more teeth were extracted, two from each side. This left me with two teeth in my upper gum and gapping holes in the line up of my upper teeth. I wore the ugliest pair of glasses, had an oversized mouth, poor posture, and overly short hair. There was not much to be said for my self-image at the age of twelve.

When I started to menstruate, things changed very rapidly. The eye doctor said that I had outgrown my stigmatism and no long had to wear the ugly glasses. My teeth slowly came down and almost totally filled the gapping holes in my teeth, I let my hair grow longer, much to the irritation of Aunt

Elise, and I almost grew into my mouth. All of this took a couple of years, which is normal for most children, and then the final result terrified Aunt Elise.

My breast did not grow to a nice size 34 B, but rather a rotund 36 C. I had a 23-inch waist, 36-inch hips and long slender legs. My eyes were green, set inside high cheekbones, a large full mouth and blonde hair. I did not see myself as pretty but Aunt Elise did and so did the young boys that were about to come into my life at the age of fourteen.

Danielle came home from school one day with the announcement that a new family was moving into the Wilson's old house which was three houses away from ours. The homes were located on a secondary road that formed a small subdivision of six homes. Ours was the largest of the six and was located at the end of the road where it dead-ended.

"They have a boy your age Charlie," Danielle said. "He's six foot tall, has dark hair and he's an athlete."

Danielle knew this because she had met and befriended the boy's older sister at school. In Mattoon we had only one high school, but two junior highs and the boy and I attended different junior high schools. Danielle thought that I should go with her to meet this boy so she and I walked to his house and she introduced me to him.

"Charlie this is Jerry, Jerry this is Charlie," she introduced us.

Our first introduction was a bit awkward and we had little to say to one another, but he was as tall as she had predicted, and the hairiest fourteen-year old I had ever seen! He had a full-face growth of hair that was clean-shaven and I could see chest hair peeking out the top of his shirt. He was not poster boy material, but he had kind big brown eyes, he was courteous and attentive and I decided that I liked him immediately.

I wandered what he was thinking about me

We said all the cordial things that people say when they are first introduced and I returned home with feelings of satisfaction and the hope that I had made a new friend.

It was springtime and my friends and I went to the district track meet where I knew Jerry was to be competing in the shot put. Jerry was not only tall and hairy, but he had girth and I was certain he could throw the weighty object a very long way. I was right.

Also present were all of Jerry's friends, and my friends and I thought that we had found the adolescent girls dream come true. The flirtations began and Brian, Kodie, Barry, and Jerry, thought that they too had found the ultimate in fresh meat. Jerry introduced me to his friends, and I introduced my friends to him and his friends. We all socialized between events and Kodie went to great extremes to impress us. He was already a legend in his own mind and an incurable show off.

He was very stocky and well built for a fourteen-year old. He was confident, even arrogant for one so young and he was a very good athlete. He placed well in his events that day, as did Jerry. We all had a wonderful day and I was happy for having met new people, or more truthfully 'boys'. I went home feeling giddy and said not a word to Aunt Elise about my new friends. I had a feeling that the less that she knew about my newly found friends, the better off I would be.

My secret was short lived however. To my surprise a day or two later, Jerry whom I was only beginning to know came to my house. Kodie and Brian accompanied him. I asked them to come in and quickly escorted them to the poolroom in the basement, away from the watchful eyes of Aunt Elise. Once in the basement, the boys quickly picked up cues and began to play pool.
"You look like Bridget Bardeau," Kodie said to me.
"No I don't," I said, having not a clue what she looked like.
"Ya, ya, you do," he insisted. "Don't you guys think she looks like Bridget?"
"Oh ya, you do," chimed in Brian.
I was feeling really flattered by all of this. I knew that Bridget Bardeau was famous and beautiful, but that was all, and these guys think I look like her.
"You have a really nice home," Kodie said. "You're rich."
It was obvious that Aunt Elise and Uncle Howard were successful because of the many amenities that surrounded us, but I found this to be embarrassing and didn't want to talk about it.
"No we're not rich; we just have a big house." I said.
"You're rich," he reiterated.
I did not respond.

I left the poolroom and went to the adjacent room that was an activities / playroom with an office desk and a fireplace. Kodie stopped playing pool and followed me to this room. Without uttering another single word, he approached me and put his arms around me. He put his mouth over mine, his tongue flickering in and out of my mouth, then probing deeper and then flickering again. Then suddenly he stopped the flickering altogether, his kiss now probed to new depths as he taught me about passion and the power of a kiss. He had clearly done this before although I had not. I was mesmerized and forever changed. I never dreamt in all of my fantasies that the rush of a kiss could be so be consuming. I think that was the very moment that I fell in love with him.

It seemed for several weeks that Kodie was at Jerry's house more often than his own and inevitably the two boys would find their way to my house. Aunt Elise and Uncle Howard were away at work and I was free to pursue my interests with these two new companions.
Kodie and I would find ourselves in the basement where there were no watchful eyes and I would bask in his arms and his soul touching kisses. We moved to the basement bedroom where the passion escalated and I found him touching me in places no one had ever touched me before. I knew that I should not be allowing him to do this but I didn't care.
When he kissed me and touched me like that, my heart sang and I was filled with delight.
I had finally found something that I thought would fill that empty cavern in my heart. The cavern was a deep empty hole left by maternal abandonment, and if I listened closely I could almost hear the lonely whine of the wind blowing through the hollowness; but when Kodie kissed me the lonely howl stopped. My heart felt full for the first time in many years.

I was entirely too young for this deep and meaningful relationship and I was overwhelmed by the new found attention that I was now receiving. Consequently, when Kodie was not around, and Jerry was, I attempted to find the same euphoria with Jerry that I had found with Kodie.
Jerry asked me one day, "Wanna sit on my lap and talk about the first thing that pops up?"
With an adolescent giggle, I sat on Jerry's lap.

We laughed and cut up and I kissed Jerry, but it wasn't the same. It wasn't Kodie.

I don't remember if I told Kodie about Jerry, or if Jerry did, but Kodie was livid with me when he learned that I had been entertaining the idea of pursuing Jerry.

"You want dumpy old Jerry, you can have him!" Kodie had said indignantly.

"No, I don't, I want you," I cried.

Kodie's ego was far too big for this insult and there was nothing I could do to right the wrong that I had committed. He was a lover boy in his own mind and I had insulted him and his precious ego. Suddenly Kodie, his delicious kisses and his empowering touch were all gone, and I had left myself again with the cavern in my heart. It took many years before I understood why I sabotaged my own relationships.

Jerry and I on the other hand became the best of friends. I sat on his lap nearly everyday and I kissed him on the lips when I said hello and goodbye. I asked him and his parents to come to our house for the Fourth of July that summer to see the fireworks that Uncle Howard set off each year, and the two of us grew inseparable. Although I had girlfriends too, Jerry became my very best friend, and we began to make plans early for our journey together to California after our high school graduation. I was going to see my mother!

Aunt Elise did not approve of Jerry at first. She did not believe that a fourteen-year old could possibly be that hairy, and that big, but he truly was. At the time that Kodie was hanging around she did not put much stock in him, assuming that he was just another kid in her house, but that would change in a few short months. Jerry and I continued to hang out together, doing things that kids that age do. We went for ice cream together, played basketball in the driveway, talked on the phone, listened to music, but we did not pursue a romantic relationship. We both knew that it was not right for us, and I was still obsessed with Kodie, the love that I had thrown away.

In the fall of that year, Aunt Elise and Uncle Howard went to Portugal for vacation and left the children at home. I was functioning under the supervision of Clarice and Danielle who were both in high school. We were to be on good behavior while our parents were away and not give them a hard time.

Jerry came down one evening while my parents were gone and to my astonishment, he had Kodie and Brian with him. I think Kodie had talked Jerry into coming to my house when he learned my parents were not home. The three of us sat at the table in the family room drinking cola and talking while we listened to the radio. Suddenly Kodie asked to speak to me privately. I joyfully took him to my bedroom that was upstairs directly over the family room. I was so hopeful that he had reconsidered, and wanted me back again.

As we entered the bedroom, he shut and locked the door behind us. He embraced me and began kissing me the way that only he could do. We lay on the bed and continued to neck, as the erotica built between us. He began to remove my clothes and attempted to caress my breasts and I shoved his hands away.
"What's wrong with you?" he asked. "You wanted this before."
"I wanted it before because I believed that you wanted me." I answered. "I don't think you want me now, you just want to get in my pants tonight."
"No," he said breathlessly between kisses, "I want you."
"Well I don't want you," I said as I attempted to push him off of me.
He was not yielding. In fact he became more aggressive, pushing my sweater up over my breasts, pulling my bra aside and trying to cup my breast. I fought his advances and broke free from him. I bolted for the door but he grabbed me and pushed me back on to the bed.
He remounted me and began to attempt to kiss me again, all the while groping and attempting to undress me.
"I don't want this Kodie! Let me go!" I said between clinched teeth.
I managed to roll over and shove him to the floor, and again I bolted for the door. Once again he caught me and dragged me back to the bed. This happened numerous times before I actually got to the door and got away from him.

I ran down stairs to where Jerry and Brian were trying to figure out what we were doing up there to cause the light fixtures to rattle from the ceiling. I was traumatized and not laughing. My sweater was no longer tucked in to

my jeans, and my jeans were partially unzipped, my hair was a mess, but mostly my tender young heart was shattered.
"He tried to rape me," I said on the brink of tears, "just get him out of here,"
Jerry, Kodie and Brian departed soon thereafter.

The very next evening I was back at Jerry's house. This time Jerry's parents were not at home and Brian and Barry were there. I was extremely upset still, and I wanted one of these guys to explain to me why Kodie had done that to me. Their responses were all the same.
"He's an asshole, Charlie," Brian said.
"He's not worth you losing sleep over, forget him!" Barry said.
"I told you a long time ago that he's a jerk, didn't I?" Jerry asked.
None of these explanations did anything to ease my grief, and since Jerry's parents were not home and the three of them were already in the booze cabinet, I decided to drink too.
As it turned out Brian was mourning the loss of his girlfriend Kathy, who had just broken up with him, and I was wallowing in my own self-pity. What better reason to drink.
Jerry was tending the bar and none of us knew how to pour a real drink so he started filling water glasses with 'suicides'. A suicide is a shot of everything in the cabinet. It didn't take more than one drink a piece, since there was nothing in the glasses but straight alcohol, and after each of us had drunk our drink we were extremely intoxicated. It's a small wonder that one of us did not end up in the emergency room with alcohol poisoning, but we did not. After getting good and drunk, the four of us waddled to my house.
When we arrived at my house, Clarice and Danielle were beside themselves. Here were four fourteen year olds drunk as skunks and all over the house. Brian had gotten to my bedroom window where he was trying to climb out to kill him self, because Kathy didn't love him anymore. Jerry was into my parents booze cabinet where he was still mixing drinks, I was in the upstairs bathroom throwing up and Barry was trying to make out with me while I puked.
I have no memory of how Clarice and Danielle finally got the three boys out of the house and the situation under control, but eventually they did.
The following morning, I learned what a hang over is, but I had bigger problems than a broken heart and a headache. I had blue jean stains all over

the wall under my bedroom window and a serious shortage of vodka in the booze cabinet. If that wasn't bad enough there was not a single person of age in our house that could replenish the missing vodka.

I decided that my life was over so I swallowed a handful of aspirin and waited for death.

Of course death did not come, but the dry heaves did. I was as sick as I had ever been, my heart was broken, and boy was Aunt Elise going to be pissed! I was frightened.

When Uncle Howard and Aunt Elise returned from Portugal, I had no choice but to face her wrath. Neither of them drank excessively, but they shared cocktails every evening. I knew that she would have checked the alcohol levels in each bottle before she left and clearly there was a large volume of vodka no longer in the bottle.

She called me to their bedroom where there were recliners for each of them. I nervously sat on the edge of Uncle Howard's chair and waited for the death sentence.

"Would you like to tell me why my vodka bottle is so low?" she asked me very sternly.

"Because Jerry, some friends and I drank it." I said with fear in my voice.

"I understand that all of you were already drunk when you arrived here." She said.

"Ya, we started drinking at Jerry's house. Jim and Helen weren't home," I quickly and earnestly replied.

"Why at your age were you drinking at all?" she asked me, her voice raising an octave.

Here it comes, my death sentence. What is she going to do to me? I sat frozen in that chair, but the truth came spilling out of my mouth.

"Kodie was here the night before, and he molested me and he wouldn't let me out of my room and he kept trying to pull my clothes off of me, and I tried to get away and he kept grabbing me and dragging me back to the bed." I said not even believing that I was telling her this.

Her voice softened, she squinted her eyes slightly, and then she asked me, "Who did this to you?"

"Kodie," I said, "the boy that was here last spring and early summer." I was wrenching my hands as I said this. I was probably going to be in trouble for letting the boys in the house now too.

She asked me, "Was that the sandy haired, short-stalky kid that came down here with Jerry?"

I just nodded my head.

"He did not rape you did he?" she asked,

"No, he just wouldn't stop when I asked him to over and over. Then when I tried to get away he kept grabbing me and trying again and again. I finally got away, but I was so upset that I went to Jerry's and drank the next day."

I think Aunt Elise felt somewhat responsible for the near rape in her own home because she was on another continent. She softened greatly with the telling of my near rape experience.

"You should not have been drinking she said, and you should not have brought those boys to our home either in our absence or under the influence," She said "but I understand how you must have felt after that boy did that to you."

I sat silently in the chair, looking at my hands in my lap and said nothing.

"You are grounded from all activities and the telephone for a month," she said, "Do you understand me?"

I nodded my head and left the sentencing room. All things considered I thought I had gotten off pretty easily. I think Kodie got off even easier. Aunt Elise did not take sexual offenses lightly. Had we not both been fourteen years old, I think she would have pressed charges, if he had actually raped me, I know that she would have.

Chapter 8

What Kodie and I did to one another's reputations after this incident is absolutely deplorable. Kodie told anyone who would listen that he had 'scored big' with me. I told anyone who would listen that he was a molester and not to be trusted. Consequently we both lost a great deal. He could not find a girl that was willing to go out on a date with him, and I was labeled a loose girl that anyone could bed. It was a very tough label to live up to as a virgin, but I'm sure that Kodie was having no fun either with his new role as a sex offender.

I did not realize the full magnitude of what he had done to my reputation until Mitch had a friend over by the name of Nick. It was customary for new comers to get a grand tour of our home. My aunt and uncle had worked hard for this achievement, both of them having risen above near poverty levels in their childhoods and they were proud of it. So Mitch was fulfilling this family tradition. He had probably already shown Nick the full finished basement, the main floor with the formal dining and living room, the family room and kitchen, the back hall bathroom, laundry room, and garage. He had now brought Nick upstairs to where the remaining three bedrooms as well as the master suite and two additional bathrooms were located.

He opened the door to my bedroom where I shared a bed with Donna, She and I were already in our pajamas and in bed although not yet asleep. He turned on the light at the switch and proceeded to introduce us.
"This is my little sister Donna's room and where the whore sleeps." He said.
I was astonished that Mitch would say that about me! There he stood at my bedroom door with one of the cutest guys he had ever brought home and he introduced me as a whore!
"Go to hell Mitch!" I said, and then I turned my attention to this very handsome Italian friend of his. I smiled my sweetest smile and simply said, "Hi."
"Hi" he responded, "It's nice to meet you."
He and Mitch left my room and continued their tour through the house.

The following morning I found Nick downstairs in the family room when I entered in my pajamas. He had spent the night with Mitch and I didn't know it.

"Good morning," he said when I entered the room, a playful grin on his lips.

'Oh my God! I have morning breath, my hair is a wreck, I have no make up on,' I thought to myself,

"Good morning," I responded, and I quickly retreated back upstairs to correct the undone vanities.

Royce and I were very close. He and I had shared the same grade level since the time that we entered kindergarten together. So later that day, after I had reentered the family room and the vanities had been tended to, I approached Royce and asked him why Mitch was so angry with me, and saying such terrible things about me.

"He's been listening to locker room talk." Royce said.

"What locker room talk?" I demanded.

"Kodie has told everyone that he felt you up, laid you and that you gave him a blowjob." Royce calmly responded.

"I absolutely did not! I exclaimed. "I can't believe he is saying that stuff about me."

"Well he's saying it and the guys in the locker room believe it, even Mitch." Royce said.

I was absolutely distraught over these lies. I went to Mitch and told him that they were all lies, but he did not believe me.

Mitch had a terrible chip on his shoulder and a lot of his anger was not generated by my conduct or my reputation. He picked on all the children in the home, especially Royce because he was such a runt. Mitch liked to spit on his finger and stick in our ears because it made us so angry. He was slightly overweight and a bully. Much bigger than the rest of us, he simply antagonized someone every chance he got, but his obvious contempt for me was different. He really believed everything that he had heard in the locker room and he really believed that I had done all of the things that Kodie said that I had done.

Not surprisingly, Nick thought I might be worth pursuing.

I was still in junior high and not allowed to date until I was sixteen. Nick was already sixteen and attended at the high school. He had his driver license and a car so it was easy for me to sneak away with him during high school sporting events. I would go to the gymnasium and watch the basketball game until half time. At half time Nick would play his trumpet with the band and then the two of us would leave in his car and go to another one of his friend's house. This friends name was Jerry, but Nick called him Slick. In exchange, Slick called Nick the WOP. This absolutely infuriated Nick's father when he heard his son being called this.

At Slicks house, or in his car, Nick was always trying to get me to have sex with him. I refused him time and time again.
"Come on," he would say, "you'll like it I promise."
"I'm not ready yet," I told him.
I enjoyed his kisses and I allowed him to touch me intimately, but I was not ready to validate Kodie's accusations.
"Do you know how it feels to have my own brother say those things about me?" I once asked Nick. "I hate it, and I don't deserve it. I'm still a virgin and Mitch calls me a whore."
"Mitch is a moron," Nick said, "I know you're not a whore."
It was a valiant effort on Nick's part but I was not budging. I believed myself to be head over heels in love with him, but I still was not ready to loose my virginity and further damage my reputation. In utter frustration Nick diligently persisted without success, but he did not stop seeing me. Our relationship continued this way for two solid months.

I had his name plastered all over my notebook at school. My biology teacher who had taught Clarice, Danielle, Mitch, and now Royce and I, noticed Nick's first and last name on my notebook. He became immediately concerned. He had never met the boy but Nick's reputation had reached that level at my middle school. Apparently, Nick had bedded a young girl the previous year and one of the staff members had overheard the girl talking about it in the girls' restroom. This was shared with the entire faculty in the teachers lounge and my biology teacher did not forget the name. In his own way he had grown fond of our family.

Every year he saw the same insect collection but with new additions each year. After Donna used the collection and she would be the last in our home to need it, he asked if he could keep it. Of course we gave it him.

At this time however he was not concerned about insects, but an Italian boy that perceived him self to be a 'Casanova.' My teacher did not contact Aunt Elise but he did go to Royce and ask him to speak to me.
"I noticed his name on her notebook," he said. "That boy is trouble and Charlie does not need to be with him. He has already caused heartache to another girl last year when he talked her into having sex."
Royce said that I was crazy about him, but that he would deliver the information.
When we got home from school that day, Royce came to me and told me what our biology teacher had said. I listened to what he had to say but it had no impact. I was right back in Nick's car the following Friday.

Nick and I went to Slick's house again. While Nick was out of the room, Slick approached me and wanted to speak with me privately.
"Charlie he does not love you, he only wants to take you to bed. Don't give him what he wants, he will only hurt you," he said.
"I'm not going to Slick, really I'm not." I responded.
Slick seemed satisfied but I was not overly convinced that his intentions were honorable. I had suspicions that Slick had a crush on me and was trying to sabotage my relationship with Nick. I liked Slick a lot but not that way, he was just a good friend.

Nick persisted in trying to get me into bed but I persisted in refusing him.
"Nick, I am not going to give Mitch more ammunition. He calls me a whore and a bitch all the time. I think he has forgotten my name because he never uses it. I don't deserve to be called those things and I'm tired of him saying those things to me." I said with conviction. Nick knew that I was not going to weaken, at least not this night.
He sat back on the sofa released a heavy sighed, put his arm around me leaned toward me and kissed me on the cheek.

The following Monday, Mitch came home from school and apologized to me.

"I'm sorry for all the things that I have been saying to you." He said. "I know you're really not a whore, and you don't put out."
I was flabbergasted! "What happened to you?" I asked.
"Nick cornered me at school and told me to stop calling you names." He said.
"Really?" again I was flabbergasted even more.
"Ya, he said that he thinks you are still a virgin and that you didn't do any of those things that Kodie said you did."
"I didn't!" I said indignantly.
"I know," he said, "and I'm sorry."
I think Nick really got a hold of Mitch and threatened to 'kick the shit out of him' if he didn't stop calling me names. Not only was it unfair to me but also it was really screwing up his efforts to seduce me. Additionally this action allowed me to place more trust in him.

From that day forward, Mitch and I bonded. No one was ever going to call me a bitch again if it was within his earshot.

One week before my fifteenth birthday I walked into the house after a basketball game.
Danielle took one look at me and she did not ask, she stated, "You got laid tonight."
I don't know how she knew but she knew. Perhaps all the innocence had left my eyes.
What ever she saw there in my eyes, it was not happiness. I hated the entire experience.
The Italian Stallion that Nick thought himself to be was a myth in his own mind. He was not gentle, his love making skills were lacking and he came into me like a Brahma bull. Loosing my virginity had been almost as sexually satisfying as a root canal.

I did not terminate our relationship immediately though. I attempted on one or two more occasions to perform for him but I simply found myself not wanting his penis to penetrate me.
"I can't do this," I finally said to him, "it is not what I want."
"Well it is what I want," he said, and at that point our short relationship was over. Even though I believed myself to be in love with him, I was relieved

when the demands for performance ended. His kisses did not curl my toes as Kodie's had, my insides did not wreath with ecstasy, and my physical being did not long for him to penetrate me as it had with Kodie. I had not acted on those feelings with Kodie, but they were all there, even the night that he had molested me. Nick's style was completely different. He had none.

It was quite some time before I would find myself willing to have intercourse again. I was not really damaged to the point that sex would become a problem in the future, but I had learned a valuable lesson. I was not ready for a sexual relationship.

The following summer I met a very nice young man that Aunt Elise and Uncle Howard approved of. He was very courteous and respectful and he was a dockhand at the marina where our new 43' houseboat was being moored. My relationship with him was just what I needed after the first two abusive relationships, and Aunt Elise liked that she could keep an eye on us. He was patient and we moved into our relationship slowly. We did many things together recreationally as well as just hanging out at the dock. He was also two years older than I was but he did not get his self worth from bedding little girls. Our relationship grew to something deeper than just dating and when he and I finally did decide to become intimate it was much less turbulent, much gentler, much less intrusive and ultimately more satisfying. I really felt loved by this young man, there for the experience did not feel degrading. I was only fifteen and still too young, but I was still always searching for that thing that would fill that gapping hole in my heart. For a while I thought this young man could do it for me.

In reality it was a yummy summer romance that I very much enjoyed, but it was not the answer to filling that hole in my heart. When the summer ended, so did the relationship
We both returned to our prospective schools in different towns, and without his constant presence and attention I became restless and began to entertain new suitors. I was now in high school and all the boys from Jerry's middle school were attending the same school that I was now attending. There was way too much fun to be had and too many jocks for me to walk the halls with for me to stay tied down to some guy twenty-five miles away.

Chapter 9

The years that followed were really uneventful. There was one boyfriend after another, dances, proms, Homecomings, new acquaintances, reuniting with old boyfriends and breaking up with them for the pursuit of new boyfriends. I was in love and out of love so many times it makes my head spin now, but it wasn't really love. In fact I now know that every time I had a successful relationship with a boy, I ended it. Then I pouted for months and obsessed over that individual as if there had never been anyone else. However, there had only been one real love ever, and that love was now taboo.

Despite the experience that I had so hated with Nick, I still believed that I was in love with him and when he asked me out as I approached my sixteenth birthday, I was elated.
I was not allowed to go on a car date until I was sixteen and I begged Aunt Elise to allow me to go.
"I'll be sixteen next week," I pleaded, "Can I go, please?"
"I think this boy has roaming hands, and rushing fingers." She said, "But I'll let you go."
"Oh, thank you!" I exclaimed.
"Be careful with this boy and don't let me learn that his glove box is a make shift refrigerator for alcoholic beverages." She had warned.
She had not a clue that he had already destroyed my virginity, and probably her weakest point of resistance is that she too found him to be incredibly handsome.

She once commented to Royce how handsome she thought Nick was.
Royce replied, "Charlie thinks so too." It was more of an over statement with a hint of humor. Royce knew I was crazy about him.

The date itself was not a very big deal. I only remember going out for pizza and while waiting for our pizza he lit a cigarette and offered one to me.
"I don't smoke." I responded.

"That's really good," he said, "you really shouldn't. I quit during the wrestling season."
Still despite his sage advice, I thought in 1974 that saying that I did not smoke was the most un-cool thing I had ever done. The following day I went straight to the store and bought my first pack of cigarettes. The first of what would be many packs for many years.

I still believed myself to be in love with this young man and we resumed a sexual relationship. Still I had not mastered the fine art of erotica mounting to orgasm and I found intercourse to be unsatisfying if not down right repulsive, particularly with this Italian Stallion that processed not a morsel of knowledge about preparing his partner.
He eventually ended the relationship because I was not a wreathing sweating participant.
The truth be known, I was not stroking his ego.

Jerry and I remained steadfast inseparable friends and found ways to get into trouble together. He introduced to me to weed and speed, and we remained drinking buddies. I rode to school with him and we got stoned together before school. He was just my best buddy.

Maybe I talked too much as most kids do, but Ellie and Clarice learned that I had drug connections. Clarice wanted a hundred hits of speed for weight control and Ellie and Joe wanted a bag of weed to experience sex under the influence. So I took it upon myself to hook them up, my only mistake is that I spent my own money in getting this transaction satisfied and then I needed money for something later.

I went to Aunt Elise and asked for money to purchase something and she asked me what happened to the money that she knew that I had just recently earned babysitting. I don't know exactly what I told her, but I know that she did not believe me. What occurred as a result of me not having my own money was heartbreaking for all of us.

The following week was Easter break from school and to my astonishment Aunt Elise thought that it would be a good idea for me to go spend my spring break with Ellie and Joe. I found this to be an excellent idea so

Through the Eyes of Betsy McCall

that I could spend time with a boy that Aunt Elise did not approve of, and she would never know that we had been together. So I eagerly packed up my belongings and off to Ellie's and Joe's I went. My beau came as I'd anticipated and Joe took me riding on his motorcycle. I had a marvelous visit right up until Aunt Elise called.
The phone rang and Ellie answered it.
"Hello."
There was no return greeting from Aunt Elise, "Ellie, did Charletta provide you and Joe with marijuana?" She asked in a commanding voice.
Ellie stammered and stuttered for a moment. At first she did not reply.
Aunt Elise prompted her for an answer, "Well did she?"
Ellie knew she had no where to run so she timidly conceded that I had
"You and Joe had better get you asses over hear now and bring Charletta with you!" she barked over the telephone.

Ellie was almost trembling as she hung up the phone and revealed that Aunt Elise had learned of our mischief. I gathered my things as we prepared to leave and Joe went and retrieved the remaining marijuana. As we left their home Joe was dumping the weed bag out of the car window and stating his fear that Aunt Elise would prosecute if they were caught with it. Joe's paranoia was growing by the minute.

When we arrived at Aunt Elise and Uncle Howard's home, we were surprised to find the entire family sitting at our nine-foot dining table. The table was custom made when their family grew from seven to ten people nearly eleven years before. It had to be brought in through a picture widow and years later had to be cut up to remove it from the house. Sitting at that table was Clarice, her husband Bo, Danielle, Mitch, Royce, Donna, Uncle Howard, and of course the matriarch, Aunt Elise.

My legs were almost trembling and I truly believed that my life was over. Aunt Elise was going to kill me with her bare hands, I was sure of it. If she didn't kill me, I would never have a life again until I was in my mid twenties! I was truly terrified.

The session began.

She looked at Clarice and Bo. "Did you ask Charletta to get you speed?" Silence fell on the room.

Aunt Elise bellowed the question again, "Did you ask her to get the speed for you?"

"Yes," Clarice responded timidly, "I just wanted it to loose weight."

Aunt Elise looked momentarily satisfied, then turned to Ellie and Joe.

"Did you ask her to get you marijuana?" she asked Joe and Ellie, her voice rising a pitch with every question.

Ellie was already crying. She was feeling afraid, shame, guilt and she had lost her beloved Aunt Elise's approval. She simply nodded through her tears. Joe said nothing.

"Let me tell the two of you something and don't you ever forget it," she said through clenched teeth, "you don't live under my roof anymore, and if you want to use illegal drugs, that is your prerogative, I can do nothing about that, but" as her voice rose to another octave, she finished shouting at the four of them, "she is a minor and she does live under my roof and *you* will find another way to obtain your drugs if you feel that you need them. Is that clear?" she ranted.

Both women, now sobbing, simply nodded as their husbands bobbed their heads in unison.

Then she turned to me. This was it, the end was near, oh God in heaven what was she going to do to me. I was road kill, dead meat, my life was over.

"In your absence I took everyone of these kids to my room and interrogated them to find out what you have been doing with your money. Poor Royce here cracked because he knew it all. He tried to tell me at first that you spent it on cigarettes, but at 50 cents a pack I could not buy that. I also know that you were up all night before a school day fidgeting in your room. He finally broke down and told me the truth that you are buying, using and supplying drugs to these two." She said as she tossed her head in the general direction of my sisters.

Then very suddenly her whole demeanor changed and she was no longer a charging bull but a wounded sparrow. Her eyes filled with tears and through her tears she softly choked out these words that changed my life forever, "If you have to do drugs to deal with whatever troubles you, then I am a failure as a parent."

I sat there in total disbelief. I had broken her and reduced her to tears. The strongest most disciplined woman I had ever met was devastated by my misconduct. She was not angry, she was crushed and I had done this. Suddenly I realized that I was not relieved, 'beat me, yell at me, ground me, lock me in my room, but don't do this to me!' my mind screamed.
This was much worse than any punishment she could have thought of.
I was now reduced to an emotional basket case myself and every single female in attendance was crying hysterically.
Through my tears I finally wailed, "You have not failed me, I have failed you!"
I got up from the chair where I had been seated awaiting my sentencing.
I walked over to her, I opened my arms and hugged her with all the hugs that I had denied us both all of those years, and I knew in that moment that I loved my Aunt Elise more than I could have ever imagined. On that day, after so many years of discord and denial I realized that I'd had a mother all along I had just refused to accept her in my heart. My loyalty to my biological mother had just been too great for me to accept the love from another.

I didn't realize all of that on that day, but I did realize that Aunt Elise was a good, kind and loving woman, that loved me as if she had given birth to me. I realized that she had and was trying to do her best for me and from that day forward we bonded. No longer did I avoid her, we actually did things together and I was not afraid to approach her when I had a problem that needed parental advice.

I finally realized that I had something that few other people have. I had two mothers!

Chapter 10

Although much of the animosity was behind us, Aunt Elise was still in control and I was still a teenager with many secrets to harbor. At the age of sixteen when it became legal for me to get on birth control without parental consent, I did so through the Planned Parenthood. I took myself to this run down building in the neighboring town of Charleston (where Ellie lived) and had my first pap and pelvic and got my first packet of birth control pills. I could get them for next to nothing but it was a pain to get over there to get them so I got three months supply at a time. Feeling safe now to have sex, I did so freely. Did I need to be in love? I thought I was most of the time but I was really on a mission; I still had a cavern in my heart that I needed to fill and I eroticized that need. At the age of sixteen I was now far too mature to recognize those feeling as infantile and a longing for maternal abandonment that could now never be filled. I had sex instead.
Admittedly it was not physically satisfying, but it seemed to fill some need.

I was now smoking regularly much to the irritation of Aunt Elise, but there was not much that she could do about it. She couldn't follow me around all the time and stop me from buying them. All she could really do was go through my personal belongings and steal them, which she did with regularity. Then I would simply go steal hers when I had none. The really weird thing is that we never spoke of the thefts.

She also had this belief that a woman could not wear a tampon. She had a hysterectomy at an early age, but prior to that she had never been able to use them. They were probably miserable in those pioneering days, but by the time I was a consumer I could not figure out what the dilemma was all about. All she ever bought were pads, so I took it upon myself to buy my own tampons. I came home one evening with a paper bag and set it on the steps going upstairs that led to my bedroom and bathroom.
"What's in the bag?" she asked
"Feminine hygiene things," I responded.

She finished the task that she was doing in the kitchen, and then went to the bag to inspect its contents. True to my words, that is all that she found was a package of tampons.

"I don't know how you girls wear those things, I never could," she said.

"I have no problems with them and they are a lot more comfortable," I responded.

That was the end of that conversation.

She simply did not trust me and she was obviously checking to see if what I had told her was true, after all we stole one another's cigarettes all the time.

Then one night in my sophomore year of high school over Christmas break I asked if I could go to a New Years Eve party with Mitch.

"With all these holiday parties there is probably going to be a massive outbreak of teen pregnancies this year." Responded Uncle Howard.

"Ya," responded Aunt Elise, "but Charletta doesn't need to worry because she's on the pill."

My mouth fell open and I sat there simply looking at them.

'How in the hell did they know that?'

I responded the only way I could. "Can I go to the party or not?"

"As long as your going with Mitch I suppose it's alright," responded Aunt Elise.

Of course she would know, she was constantly going through my things, my room, my purse, but she wasn't finding what she was really looking for. She was finding things that surprised her but not drugs. I think this pleased her.

As it turned out Mitch was the bad boy that night. He drank entirely too much. I had a firecracker go off in my face that temporarily blinded and deafened me at the stoke of midnight, but Mitch was running up and down the rural road at speeds in access of sixty miles per hour and he was out of control. He dented both front panels of his Opal GT as he ran in and out the ditches and I stood on the side of the road screaming with tears running down my cheeks for someone to stop him. Eventually we got him out of the car and had to make arrangements for friends to get us home. I did not have the ability to drive a stick shift and was still not licensed. We got home eventually and Mitch licked his wounds as well as those on his sporty new / used car that he had only recently repainted.

Chapter 11

At the close of my sophomore year, Mitch was off to the army. We were in peace times fortunately so I was not so terrified as I'd been when Boyd went to Vietnam. Mitch was off to get an education in nursing which left me wondering what I would do after graduation.

"I think I would like to be an airline stewardess," I had shared with Aunt Elise.
"No you don't want to be an airline stewardess," she responded, "they are nothing more than glorified waitresses."
"Ok," I responded, "then what should I pursue?" Not feeling overly passionate about any career goals.
"I think you should become a model," she replied.
"I'm not pretty enough to become a model!" I exclaimed nervously laughing that notion off.
"But you are," she said "and you are incredibly photogenic."

I basically had no sense of self worth and certainly did not see in the mirror what ever it was that she saw. I was leery of this recommendation but I mulled it around. I now look back on pictures of me at that time in my life and see what it was that she saw. She was right.

In the mean time I had an encounter with a man ten years older than I was (one of my unsatisfying sexual partners) soon after that and I shared with him that I was contemplating modeling as a career after high school.
"What do you think Al?" I asked as I lay beside him in his bed.
"I think you have entirely too big a breast to be a model." He had responded. "Models have no boobs, just look in any magazine."
I took him at his word and decided to never set myself up for rejection because my breast were too big.

What ever would I become? I was destined to be a housewife and mother, because I already knew that I was dumb, I had been told that since childhood. How could anyone that had failed kindergarten ever grow up to be someone important? Certainly not me, and that was the end of my modeling aspirations.

What annoys me the most is that Al is probably a bar patron that sits on the same stool today, in the same pub, that he sat in when I met him thirty years ago. To me he was a mature man with wisdom; today I know that he was nobody and possessed all the wisdom of a housefly.

I went into my senior year of high school with absolutely no idea or concern for what I would do the following year. I had no feel for my future or for that matter any real interest. I would find a good man to take care of me and take me where I wanted to go and he would do what I wanted him to do. That was my life's goal.

Before I could get married and create this wonderful life however, I had another goal and that was to go to California with Jerry to reconcile with my mother. That was my goal for the year of 1976. I had no idea how disrupted that unrealistic dream would become in the months ahead. My final year of high school was to be a devastating year of tragedies that would change my life once again.

Ironically I started my period on New Years Day in 1976, and my Air Force boyfriend had broken up with me. I found that to be somewhat devastating, but I always did when I was the one who had been dumped instead of being the dumpee. Rejection always sent me on a quest of trying to make that person love me again. It was a cycle of self-sabotage. If the other person was theoretically in love with me, then I became bored with the relationship and had to do something to create stimulus; there for I would somehow do something to cause the other person to step out of the relationship and then I would obsess to get that person to love me again. So on this New Years Day I was licking my wounds again and obsessing about my air force flame.

Eventually he came back to me and eventually I became bored again. This time when I became bored I did not break up with him. He was at the Air Force base where he commuted back to see me as frequently as possible and I had too much time on my hands. It was in January of that year that I reunited with Kodie.

I was standing at the door to my algebra class when I saw him coming down the hall to his drama class across the hall. He was wearing a sheet draped around him as if he was Julius Caesar and I could see his thick and powerful thigh on one leg. His chest was exposed on the other side and I could not help but notice how incredibly buff he looked. I felt stimulated just looking at him. At that moment I made the decision that I was going to seduce him and that is exactly what I did.

I initiated the reconciliation and it wasn't long before I was in his dad's car and we were having sex. He had reservations, but I insisted! I wanted him as I had never wanted any other male in my life.
"My dad told me when I left not to leave tracks in his car." Kodie said laughingly.
"Shut up and make love to me," I responded.
He did just that. It was not what I was hoping for since it was in a car, but I had gotten my way and I had sex with the love of my life after five years, and still his kisses curled my toes.

Six weeks later I could not stomach a hamburger, a cigarette made me nauseous, and the smell of a man's cigar nearly killed me when I was at the mall. Aunt Elise and Uncle Howard were in Hawaii visiting Mitch when I went to the family physician and had a pregnancy test. It was positive; I was pregnant with Kodie's fetus.

I made a fatal mistake, I told Kodie. I don't know if he thought he was going to marry me, or what his noble intentions were and I'll never know because he never had the chance to tell me.

Aunt Elise and Uncle Howard returned from their trip.
I entered their bedroom where Aunt Elise was sitting in her recliner. I sat in Uncle Howard's recliner and said, "I need to talk to you about something." She looked at me and waited for more information.
"I'm pregnant." I simply stated.
"I thought you were on the pill?" she asked incredulously.
"I was, but my script ran out and I just didn't get back to the clinic for my annual." I responded.

"Who is the father might I ask?"
This was a tough question because I knew that she had not forgotten the assault four years earlier.
"Kodie," I simply stated.
She looked momentarily confused.
"That arrogant little bastard that molested you?" she asked in amazement.
"We were kids then." I responded.
"You were kids then? You're kids now!" she stated with exasperation in her voice.
"It's OK," I said, "I want to carry the baby to term. I'll go live with grandma in Oklahoma, I'll go to school down there and I'll give the baby up for adoption.
"No you won't. You will wonder everyday of your life where your baby is, you will wonder if it was a boy or girl and it will never stop haunting you. You will have an abortion, and that is the end of it." She flatly stated.
"I don't want to have an abortion," I cried out.
"You are not having a baby," she said without diplomacy. "I am going to burn in hell for the sins of my daughters." She was referring to Danielle's abortion that had taken place two years earlier as well as my current dilemma.

True to her word I was in the abortion clinic before the week was out. It was the most horrid experience of my life. I laid on a table in a stark white room, the dilation of my cervix was nauseating and the extraction of my fetus was excruciatingly painful, but the physical pain was miniscule compared to the emotional suffering. Following the evacuation of my fetus, I was left on the table alone with a glass jar that contained the remains of my unborn child. I had lost a precious part of myself and the anguish of that loss left me consumed with grief. I laid there alone in that room, staring at that jar, as tears streamed down my face.

However, I was not the only one in tears that day. When I was not at school that day, Kodie went to my best friend, and asked her point blank if I was having an abortion.
"She had to, her parents made her." Toni replied.

Kodie's eyes filled with tears and he left school for the remainder of the day.

I later learned that he went to his best friends home where he cried his eyes out all day long and shared his grief with his friend and his friend's mother.

Kodie and I were not together after that. We never spoke of our loss and we went on as if nothing had ever happened, but we both knew and we both mourned.

Chapter 12

Three months later I was participating in physical education, mid day after lunch. It was one week before my high school graduation and except for final exams: we were doing as little as possible in anticipation of our freedom. Our class had dressed out in our gym clothes and had just arrived on the field to begin our work out when the instructor called out to me.
"You have been called to the principals office." She said to me.
"Why?" I asked confused.
I had done nothing wrong and the only other time I had been called to the office was when I had been caught skipping school.
"I don't know." She simply replied.
So off I went to the principals office. When I arrived I was even more confused because Danielle was standing there visibly shaken with tears in her eyes. Danielle did not belong here; she had been out of high school for three years and was working in the X-ray department at the hospital.
"What are you doing here?" I asked.
She did not mince words with me, she simply stated through her tears, "Mom's dead."
Now my confusion was exacerbated by shock.
"What do you mean, mom's dead?" I asked incredulously.
"She's dead." She stated again through her tears as she now began to lose control. "Get your things, we have to go. Ken Gauge is waiting for us."
We went to the girl's locker room together where my shaking hands somehow managed to turn the combination to the lock. My hands were trembling as I fumbled through my things and retrieved my personal belongings. A thousand questions were racing through my mind. 'What had happened, where, when?'
My hands were trembling, my breathing heavy and erratic, but the tears did not come.
"Was there an accident?" I asked with a quivering voice.
"No." Danielle responded now becoming irritated. "She's just dead, OK! Now let's go."

This did not compute. 'Aunt Elise was not ill, and she was not old.' My mind raced as we left the locker room and I carried my clothes to the awaiting vehicle.

We approached the car driven by Mr. Gauge and to my astonishment Royce was already there. He was sitting in the backseat silently with tears in his eyes and Mr. Gauge was patiently waiting behind the steering wheel. Mr. Gauge was probably wishing that he could have been having root canal surgery right at that point in time. Anything would have been better than picking up these dependants to share this horrible news.

I got into the car and the silence was deafening. Mr. Gauge was sober, Royce was silent and teary eyed and Danielle was breaking down very quickly. I could stand this no longer!

"What happened?" I managed to ask through my shock.

"We don't know yet, we only know that dad went to join her on the boat where she spent the night last night and he found her in the cuddle cabin." Danielle softly stated through her tears.

Silently we rode back to our home, none of knowing what to say to the other.

When we arrived Ellie and Clarice were already there. To this day I don't recall how Donna got home. We may have picked her up, she may have been in the car when I got in, at this point I was in total shock. I simply don't remember.

What I do remember were the droves of people, flowers, and food that just kept coming and coming and coming. The local florist must have made a fortune. I had no idea that Aunt Elise had been so loved and respected by the people in our community.

One local attorney sent the most massive floral arrangement I had seen in my entire life. His respects were two fold due to an accident involving his son a year earlier. It was very foggy and his son was in a head on collision with Danielle's boyfriend ironically. Danielle's boyfriend was in one of those old iron tanks from the fifties, and the attorney's son was in a new sporty car with only two seats. Danielle's boyfriend had a broken jaw and some minor injuries, but the attorney's son's face was literally destroyed. The local sheriff could do nothing to keep the boy from drowning in his own blood and the paramedics had not arrived yet. Wisely the Sheriff came to our home and asked Aunt Elise to help.

Aunt Elise wasted no time running for the tools that she needed as she abandoned her dinner and left with the sheriff to assist at the scene of the accident. At the scene she performed an emergency tracheotomy that saved the boys life.

Ironically while Aunt Elise was at the scene of the accident, Danielle was all pumped up and wanted to go down the road to see the wreck. Fortunately we did not do that. She would have been distraught when she learned who was in the other vehicle not to mention that we would have been severely reprimanded for getting in the way especially in that fog. Aunt Elise informed Danielle of the other driver when she returned home.

The father of that boy continued to send flowers on the anniversary of Aunt Elise's death for years to follow.

That first night was a restless night for all of us. Uncle Howard's sister had arrived from Indiana. She was a registered nurse and she administered tranquilizers to us in an effort to help us rest but they had little effect. We were coping the best way we knew how accompanied by a lot of tearful hugs.

The following day more family members arrived, planes trains and automobiles brought in Aunt Elise's brothers, her parent's and Uncle Howard's siblings and all of their children. It was becoming a very crowded house despite its size, but the people helped to keep us occupied.

Then the most emotionally challenging thing occurred. Ellie informed me that she was picking our mother up at the airport the following day.

"Mom is coming for Aunt Elise's funeral?" I asked incredulously.

I had waited for this woman to show up for thirteen years and now that Aunt Elise was dead she was suddenly going to come. Here I was stricken by grief and all of a sudden I was supposed to be elated and embrace my long lost mother?

I flipped out!

I had learned to drink beer a long time ago, and being good Catholics we had all the beer at this wake anyone could want to drink. Uncle Howard's sisters were busy in the kitchen keeping food out for everyone and we family members were stumbling around in an effort to cope, each of us in our own private little hell. I drank.

Boy did I drink and by nightfall of the second day I had become a blubbering drunk in total hysterics. I can still vaguely recall being in the basement with Boyd and screaming at the top of my lungs.
"Aunt Elise is dead!" I wailed at him with tears streaming down my face. "Aunt Elise is dead and now *she's* coming! She has no business coming to Aunt Elise's funeral! I don't want her here! Why does she have to come now?"

Boyd was growing increasingly impatient with me. "This is not the time for this," he sternly stated, "now get your self together."

My aunt's had been going through old family photos earlier in the day and had spread them out over the pool table.
"I don't want to get myself together!" I screamed as I grabbed a handful of pictures and threw them across the room. "I don't care, why does she have to come now?" I wailed.
"I don't know, and I don't care! They *were* sisters!" Boyd finally shouted. He grabbed me by my shoulders and shook me. "I don't particularly want her here either but I intend to ignore her." He flatly stated. "My mother is dead!"

"You have got to stop this and straighten up," Boyd continued, "there are a lot of people upstairs that do not need to see you like this or listen to your hysterics. Everyone here is grieving too and no one wants to see this. Do you hear me?"

Amazingly, I had heard him; Boyd had never raised his voice with me, ever. Soon after that exchange occurred I was reduced to uncontrollable tears but I had stopped the hysterical behavior. Uncle Howard's sisters gently walked me down the street to Jerry's house. Jerry's mother answered the door and she was instructed by my aunts not to let me go anywhere and for God's sake don't let me have any more to drink. Jerry's mother put her arms around me and cradled me into her home. My aunts returned to my home down the street and Jerry's wonderful mother said to me, "You are going no where tonight, but what would you like to drink honey?"

Jerry and I drank until almost dawn when exhaustion and alcohol had taken their toll. We had sat up nearly all night talking about the arrival of my mother and how frightened I was by this. She was to come with Ellie tomorrow and I really did not want to deal with this too.

The next morning I woke fairly early and truly thought I would beat Ellie and *her* to my home. I desperately wanted to be in my territory before she arrived. As I walked the block to my home from Jerry's I was confident that I had accomplished this because Ellie's car was not there. Hung over, exhausted, and somewhat ashamed of myself I timidly entered the house through the front door. I was prepared to apologize for my misconduct the previous night, but I was not prepared to walk straight into my home and lock eyes with my biological mother.

There she sat and as bad as I had dreaded this meeting with her I suddenly saw the one thing that I had starved myself for, despite the efforts of Aunt Elise to fill that void. Her eyes were full of love, the kind that only mothers know. Love, pride, and sadness for all that we had lost. She was sitting at the breakfast counter on a stool drinking coffee. She was tall and slender just as Aunt Elise her sister had been, but Aunt Elise was a bleached blonde and my mother wore a coal black wig although her hair beneath was just as black. However the thing that most struck me was the soft sadness in her eyes.

I walked over to her and she hugged me with a great bear hug. From that moment forward we bonded, but it was too little too late. I followed her around the entire time that she was with us, I sat with her at the visitation when I was avoiding the coffin with the remains of my Aunt Elise on display and eventually I began to fill her water glass with ice and straight vodka.

Boyd's survival mechanism since the day that we had left her was to ignore her and he did just that the entire time that she was there.
"I had one mother and she is dead now." He had flatly stated, and true to his word he did not acknowledge our mothers presence through her entire stay with us.

The Catholic church was packed to the rafters as we walked the center isle to the front of the sanctuary. Everything was exactly as it had been everyday of my life. Behind the alter of this magnificent old church were large ornate white castle like structures that had alcoves that resembled balconies to house statues. Jesus Christ was in the large center alcove bleeding on the cross. His mother Mary, Joseph and other sainted statues were located in other smaller alcoves. The Thirteen Stations of the Cross were mounted through out the old church on the outer walls between large stained glass windows, but the most impressive thing about this wonderful old structure were the high vaulted ceilings bearing painted imagery of biblical events and the miracles of God.

This church was ominously impressive to me when I first entered it as a five- year old child and I had studied the features on the face of Christ for the past thirteen years. Today however, none of that was important. On this day before the alter of my childhood sanctuary was the casket that held the remains of my Aunt Elise.

Nine of us made the long walk down the center isle to the first pew where we were to sit for the Mass. We were holding one another up as we made our way to our designated pew.

The mass was lovely and very long as all Catholic mass' are but this one seemed longer than most. With the closing of the mass and hearing Ave Maria, we all rose and followed the pallbearers down that long isle once more. After leaving the church we all got into our cars that were to carry us to the cemetery where Aunt Elise would be put into her final resting place. Our cars followed the hearse and car after car after car followed ours. If this had not been such a heartbreaking experience for our family, it would have been spectacular to watch. The number of family members, mourners, business owners, parishioners, and co-workers that attended her funeral was staggering. I now wonder if businesses were shut down so that the proprietors might show their respects. I am certain that an anesthetist was brought in from a neighboring town to cover for surgeries because the local hospital only had two anesthetists, one was Uncle Howard; the other was in that casket.

At the grave sight we were each given a long stem rose to toss on to the casket before it was lowered into the earth. We each took a turn to toss our rose through our tears. Danielle threw her rose and then could not break herself away. She threw herself on top of the casket and Boyd went to her side and pulled her away. It was a devastating loss to our family, but I think with the exception of Uncle Howard, Danielle took it the hardest.

After leaving the grave sight Danielle, Mitch, Royce Donna and I all got into Uncle Howard's Chrysler Imperial and headed toward our home. It was very somber in that car as Uncle Howard drove toward our home but it was in that short drive that we became aware of how incapacitated he was. He was in tears and could not keep all four tires on the road. The two right tires were off the road more often than they were on the road and we passengers were looking at one another wondering if our funerals would be next. Eventually we arrived at our home with enormous relief and joined the throng of people that were arriving to share their condolences and consume yet more food and beverages.

"I can't believe that Elise is gone, she was so young and vibrant." One of Uncle Howard's brother in laws commented.

"Charletta," my opinionated step grandmother said, "you have lost one mother and gained another, what do you think of that?"

'I think that you are a colossal idiot', is what I thought, but I smiled sweetly and said "How about that."

"A parent never expects to outlive their children," said Aunt Elise's father. "It was that diabetes that took her and she did not get that from my side of the family."
My grandparents had long since been divorced and my grandmother retorted to that indirect accusation, "Well she didn't get it from my side of the family!"
I left them to their debate over which of their lineage had carried the weak link to the pancreas. I now know that the American Indians have been suspect for the source of diabetes and if there is any foundation for that theory, then

my grandmother, whom I adored, would have lost that argument since she was ¼ Cherokee.

Whatever the link, Boyd was diagnosed in his twenties, and one of Aunt Elise's brother has it as well. It is definitely genetic and unmerciful to its victims.

What had actually caused the death of the 45 year-old Aunt Elise really remains a mystery to this day. The coroner's findings stated that her lungs had filled with fluid while she slept and he noted that her organs looked like those of a ninety-year old woman. Aunt Elise did have her share of maladies from the diabetes, weak kidneys to arthritis and a string of other aches and pains. She had taken a lot of medications over the years to combat these ailments and those medications were attributed to the premature aging of her organs. Yet despite these explanations it was still hard to comprehend when she had been seemingly well, actively participating in our home, going to work daily and alive when last I saw her.

In the few remaining days that our home was filled with relatives and well-wishers, my grandfather said something that had a profound impact on me and my future decisions.

He said, "What ever you do in your lives, please don't do anything that would bring shame to Elise."

That was a pretty tall order since I had been doing nothing but bringing shame to her for as long as I could remember.

My mother and I were together nearly every moment that she was there and I basked in her attention. She constantly complimented me and had to be touching me. She took a lot of pictures to take back to California to share with her husband and bar cronies. I think my constant attention and companionship greatly relieved some of the heartache that she suffered due to Boyd's bitterness and refusal to acknowledge her.

All too soon it was time for my mother to return to California, and then my grandparents were gone, and then another family and another and in a very short time we were left with only one another. It was a very strange time. We had no structure left and it was as if our family had developed rickets.

C. R. Perk

It was amazing that one woman had so much impact on the lives of those around her.

Royce, Donna and I returned to school to finish our final exams that our teachers were instructed to pass us on no matter what our scores, and then Royce and I graduated from high school.

A few weeks later it was Fathers Day and six of my siblings, spouses and I put all of our money together to take Uncle Howard out for dinner and dancing, the only absentee was Mitch because he was still in the army and back to his duties. Ellie was there with Joe, Boyd and Colleen, Clarice with Bo, Danielle, Royce, Donna, Uncle Howard and me. It was a time when recreation was desperately needed and this was a wonderful release for all of us.

We all had dinner and drinks, the band began to play and we ladies took turns dancing with Uncle Howard. To our astonishment they were even serving mixed drinks to Donna who was only fifteen. Perhaps it was known that we were the family that had just lost our loved one and that is why they broke all the rules for us. Perhaps it was because it was a large family gathering to honor our father. Whatever the reason, the drinks just kept coming.

"I'd like a slow comfortable screw," Royce requested.
To which the waitress replied, "Would you like that on the table or against the wall?"
Royce had no witty come back and the rest of us just went into hysterical laughter. The party was on and we were having a badly needed good time.
I ordered a black russian.
"This is pretty good," I said, "I wonder what's in it?"
I was wearing a long, low cut sleeveless gown and Boyd suggested that I go ask the bartender what's in it, "and when you do," he said "bend over real far."
"Ya right," I responded, "and he'll say boobs!"
Again the entire family went into hysterical laughter, but long after the moment was gone, Ellie was still giggling.
"Ellie it wasn't that funny," I said.

Ellie responded, "I'm not laughing at your boob joke, I'm laughing because that guy over there is laughing at us and can't take his eyes off of you."
She was pointing to a table where two young men were drinking beer and true to her words laughing and watching me.
Embarrassed I tucked my head slightly but I could not stop laughing.
He stood, approached our table. He was about six foot tall, had blue eyes, blonde hair and a dazzling smile.
"Would you like to dance?" he asked me.
To which I eagerly accepted.
As we danced he asked what the celebration was all about and I told him of our families recent loss and this was a Fathers Day pick me up for Uncle Howard.
We danced a couple of dances together and then he asked me if I'd like to go out sometime.
"Sure," I responded so we went to his car to exchange phone numbers.
He jotted my name and telephone number down on a scrap of paper that he placed on top of his car as he wrote. It was dark so I couldn't make out what type of car it was, but I knew that it was sporty and expensive.
"How about next Friday?" he asked.
"No I already have a date on Friday, how about Sunday?" I responded.
"No, Sunday isn't good for me because I have to get up early on Monday for work. How about Saturday?" he asked.
"I already have a date for Saturday." I said.
At this point he became annoyed and said, "If I have to make an appointment then just forget it!"
"No," I quickly said to him, "I'll cancel my date on Friday."
This seemed to satisfy him so having set a date we returned to the party for more drinks and dancing.

When the Fathers Day celebration ended we had spent every cent that we had pulled together for this event and Uncle Howard got saddled with the bar bill that was in excess of two hundred dollars. I think it was worth every cent to him, I know it was for the rest of us. We had successfully enjoyed ourselves and I had a met handsome young man with a sporty car by the name of Mack Hundorfer.

Chapter 13

My first date with Mack was nothing thrilling. He picked me up at my home and took me to see a movie called "Mother, Jugs and Speed." The film was very entertaining and after the movie we went out for drinks. He then took me back home and I don't recall if he even kissed me good night. It was really kind of boring and I realized that I didn't have a lot to talk with him about.

He drove a very sporty Datsun 280 Z that I found very impressive, and I learned that he worked for his dad as a truck driver-delivering tile for crop drainage. His dad owned the plant where the tile was fabricated. The tile was plastic instead of clay and carried a one hundred year warranty. In addition to the tile plant his dad also owned a sister company that imported the trenching equipment from Germany and was then sold in the United States. Both of these companies were the sole distributors in the United States, although there were dealers located through out the south and the east. Mack's dad had done well and they were well established in this miniscule spot located in the heart of the agricultural capital of the midwest. Having been raised somewhat affluent myself, I did not find the success of Mack's dad all that impressive, at least not quite yet.
Mack informed me that he had a pilot's license and asked if I'd like to go up sometime.
"I've never flown in my life." I confessed.
"Well, I'd say that it's about time you did then, huh?"
"I guess it is." I replied.
"Great, it's a date then, meet me at the airport Saturday at one o'clock and you can fly with me to Mock Falls." Mack responded.
"It's a date," I said.
I was excited and nervous. I didn't know if I would get air sick, or if I should or should not eat. Having never flown before I had no idea what to expect, but nervous or not I was going.

It was only our third date when I met Mack at the local small town airport and boarded the single propped Cessna. I was amazed by how thin the walls

were and how flimsy the aircraft felt. I sat in the passenger seat and fastened my seat belt feeling a bit apprehensive.
"Are you ready?" Mack asked.
"Let's do it," I responded.
So we taxied to the runway as Mack got clearance for take off. Before I knew it we were airborne.

The crops below were breathtaking from the sky and the beauty of it mesmerized me, I marveled that this must be the way that God sees the earth.
'Now I'm in love,' I thought to myself. ' Aunt Elise would be very pleased to know about Mack,' and the more I learned about him the more determined I was to fall in love with him. I was eighteen years old, fresh out of high school and flying around in a privately owned plane. Yes I was beginning to become impressed.

As we approached Mock Falls, Mack pulled me out of my thoughts.
"I'm not real great at landing yet, I do a lot better on take off." He said to me.
'Oh wonderful,' I thought to myself. 'Here I am in an airplane with this young man who has just admitted to having poor skills at landing a plane. What do I really know about this guy, how do I even know if he really has a pilots license at all. What if he is a nut?'

Then we began our decent. I clutched the plane door trying not to look terrified as the landing gear touched the pavement beneath us and after only a brief hop Mack brought the plane to a successful and complete stop. Feeling enormously relieved I said, "I thought you did that rather well."

"Yea, that landing was pretty smooth," he timidly admitted.

What ever we had flown up here to pick up was waiting for us at the airport. Mack retrieved it and we were back in flight and heading south once more.

We chatted about this and that on the flight back and then I asked if he was going to take me back to the airport in my hometown.
"I had Royce drive me out there and I don't have a way home." I told him.

"I'll take you home." He simply stated.
"You can't take me home in a plane, and if you land at the airport then we won't have a car." I said.
"I'll take you home," he repeated, "we're landing in Fredericks."
"There is no airport in Fredericks," I said cynically.
This was truly comical to me because I knew very well that a podunk town of twenty two hundred people could not possibly have an airport.
As we approached Fredericks and circled the landing sight I lost control of all my manners and propriety.
"You have a damn landing strip in your fucking back yard?" I asked incredulously.

Mack was embarrassed. Whether it was my abrupt use of profanity or the fact that I was overly impressed by the existence of this landing strip in his back yard, or the combination of both, it was obvious that he was uncomfortable.

He did not respond except to nod his head.

Once again on the ground, we taxied up to the house where a hanger was attached to the house. This was getting to be almost too much for me. Mack and his family were filthy rich! The home was beautifully landscaped, with a circular drive and an island in the center of the driveway. Two garages were separated by an office, and the hanger was located adjacent to the garages on the backside of the property. To the north of the property was a large shop and silos stood beyond the shop. We entered the home through the hanger into the garage and then a laundry room larger than my bedroom at Uncle Howard's home. From the laundry entrance we entered the very contemporary kitchen that was equipped with all the conveniences including an island style indoor grill and exhaust fan. The family room was adjacent to the kitchen, a long hall led to the four bedrooms to the left of the family room and kitchen. To the right of the hallway that lead to the bedrooms was another doorway that joined the foyer to the front door and to right of the door was a formal living room. Both the living room and the family room were equipped with fireplaces that were installed back to back and shared the same chimney. An atrium was located in a large window beside the front door and centered in the foyer was a circular staircase that descended to the basement.

The basement was a masterpiece in itself with a three sided fireplace that was located near the center of the largest open room, a game room equipped with pool and ping pong tables was located off to the far right of the staircase beside the large two sided bar with nine bar stools. To the right side of the fireplace was a TV room furnished with contemporary chairs and a large sofa; all of this was done tastefully in red and black including the carpet. Another bedroom was located behind the spiral staircase accompanied by a sauna and all the walls were finished in weathered barn siding.
It was not for everyone's taste but it was very well done for its time. The wallpaper behind the bar was obnoxiously loud but this was the seventies and it was very striking for that time period.

Mack's dad came into the house shortly after we arrived and I was introduced. He was a handsome man, with blonde hair sporting a mustache; he had blue eyes and appeared to be physically fit. The most prominent aura about him though was his arrogance. He didn't have to tell you how important he was because his body language said it for him. He literally reeked of self-importance, a demeanor that would not generally have been expected in an individual with an eighth grade education and had been born and raised Amish.

After meeting Mack's dad and taking a tour of the home and grounds, Mack honored his word and returned me to my home, which was about 30 miles south of Fredericks.

Soon after the flight and the tour I received the first dozen roses I had ever gotten from a guy in my life and the same day that the roses arrived Mack did a fly over Uncle Howard's home. I was so caught up in all of this and I could not believe my good fortune. 'What if I had not broken that first date with Gary to go out with Mack?'

A few months later Mack telephoned me from the air to tell me that he had just been to Florida and was on his way back home. That was when I learned of the Lear jet that was hangered at the airport in my hometown.

Soon after that call I met his dad's personal pilot for the Lear. Mack's dad served as co-pilot. The pleasant surprises seemed never to end.

I'm fairly certain that most people saw me as a gold digger, but I truly wasn't. I didn't see riches in my future. I thought I saw a life of security, contentment and fulfillment ahead of me. Most importantly I believed that Aunt Elise would have been profoundly pleased with my good fortune in finding this man, and I truly believed that he would make all of my dreams come true. He would do what ever I wanted him to do and go wherever I wanted to go and we would achieve great things together.

Mack and I were kind of mismatched because of our upbringings. I was very outgoing, outspoken and a bit rambunctious. Mack was much more resigned and had to work at being assertive. I saw him as being solid as a rock, reliable and larger than life. Three years my senior I thought he possessed the strength of Gibraltar, the courage of a lion and the Wisdom of Solomon. Was I in love with Mack or was I in love with being in love with Mack?

Mack was raised a good Christian boy and was slow to become intimate with me. However I was steadfast in my quest to get him under the sheets and he finally succumbed to my advances. We had a healthy sexual relationship. It was not earth wind and fire, but it was healthy and satisfying.

I road with him in the eighteen wheeler many times and once slipped off with him to North Carolina for two weeks while he worked at a plant there for his dad. Mack was terrified that his parents would learn of this and I was stuck in the motel room the entire time that we were there. He worried too much that he would lose his parents approval and he was constantly concealing our activities together. This seemed strange to me since he was twenty- one years old. I was only eighteen and did not feel that I had to hide from Uncle Howard. Still Mack was living at home with his parents so I took this as his way of maintaining his respect for them.

Mack would stay with me at Uncle Howard's and then get up very early in the morning and get back home and even crawl into bed before his mom realized that he had been gone all night. Uncle Howard could have cared less, he liked Mack and he knew that there was no point in preaching morality to me because he was a pioneer amongst the early believers in sexual freedom. So Mack and I continued to see one another as often as possible, usually at my home since it was safe to practice sex and quite honestly we had a lot more fun.

When we were at Mack's house I was generally bored to tears watching him watch football, baseball, or whatever sporting event happened to be in season. I did enjoy the basement though. It was where we went to drink beer, and smoke, at his mother's request. In nineteen seventy six it seemed ridiculous that we should have to go to the basement to smoke, but today it is universal for people to ask for this consideration.

Mack's mom was a simple woman of Mennonite decent. She was over weight, very domestic and profoundly meddling. She was a likable woman, very pleasant to be around but extremely opinionated. There was one way to do everything, her way.

Mack had three siblings, Sky who was thirteen, Tony who was seventeen, and his sister Paula who was a few months older than me. Paula was my favorite. She was in college getting a degree in nursing. Mack had already gotten an Associates Degree in Civil Engineering that he was not using now and the other two boys were still in middle and high school. I got the feeling that Tony did not like me much, but I also got the feeling that Tony did not like anything very much. Skye was a cute boy, still young and naïve, but of all Mack's siblings Paula had the most personality and sweetest disposition.

I have had opportunity since those early years to wonder now if Aunt Elise would have been so eager to see me in this Protestant / Catholic relationship, knowing that there were huge variances in our faiths and the structures of our childhoods. At the time however I was convinced that I was fulfilling my grandfather's wish and doing what Aunt Elise would have approved of. Consequently I was not entertaining any thoughts that Mack and I might not be suited for one another.

On November nineteenth, nineteen seventy- seven, Mack and I were married. We had a large wedding with five bridesmaids, five groomsmen, two flower girls and a Protestant wedding in Mack's childhood Mennonite church. Uncle Howard walked me down the isle and gave me away, and following the ceremony we had a proper punch and cake reception.

Uncle Howard also threatened to bellow the question "Who put the turd in the punchbowl?" knowing full well that it would be totally inappropriate, especially with the Mennonite and Amish that were in attendance.

Boyd suggested that we play 'Let's get drunk and screw' as the processional song as Uncle Howard walked me down the isle. And before the wedding, Uncle Howard was quoted as saying, "The only way this marriage is going to work is if he beats her."
Although I did not, Uncle Howard did recognize the huge differences that existed between Mack's and my life styles and personalities.

To my bitter disappointment my mother did not attend my wedding. Instead she sent me silverware for eight.

Mack and I flew to Sarasota Florida for our honeymoon. This was the winter vacationing spot for the Amish and Mennonites and a November wedding put us here at precisely that time of year. I had wanted to go on a cruise and we ended up in a small quaint sparsely furnished apartment a block away from the beach.

I spent most of the evenings pulling the threads from my underwear legs because my sisters had gotten into my bag and sewn them all shut. This was humorous although annoying and then while spending our disappointing honeymoon in this dumpy apartment, Mack decided that we needed to take his grandmother out for Thanksgiving dinner. Then to add insult to injury we also went to his mother's brothers home to have dinner with their family! This was not the way that I had anticipated spending my honeymoon, but unknown to me at the time this was simply a prelude to the future.

Chapter 14

Mack and I moved into a two-bedroom apartment which was one half of a brand new duplex. It was cute, comfortable and accommodating to our needs. It lacked the grandeur of his parent's home, but it was perfect for our newly wedded needs. Mack was no longer driving a truck and had moved to a sales position with the trenching company and was earning a base salary of eleven thousand annually plus commission, he was also provided a company vehicle. That left me with the Datsun to drive but there was nowhere to go except the laundry mat and the grocery store. I stayed pretty reclusive in the apartment and didn't go out much because every time I did go anywhere in his po-dunk little town I could hear the whispers of the residents, "That's Mack Hunsdorfer's new wife."
I never once heard one of them approach me and say "Hi, I'm Mary, welcome to our town."

If I went to one of the Amish stores the women always spoke in Dutch so I could not understand what they were saying. They may not even have been talking about me at all, but I had no way of knowing what they were talking about. I felt that everywhere I went that I was being watched, and in reality I was. I was the new girl in town and I had snagged the catch of the decade. I was Mack Hunsdorfer's new wife. I felt in those days that I was resented because I was an import. That may have actually been the case but my lack of self-esteem did nothing do alleviate the paranoia. I just felt that I was being scrutinized everywhere I went.

"They are so damn nosey!" I had complained to Uncle Howard. "They whisper behind my back and watch everything I do."
In Uncle Howard's usual maddening manner of optimism he responded, "They are interested."
"They are not interested, they are nosey and gossipy." I replied.
Uncle Howard had an uncanny way of looking at every situation with a positive attitude. Even when he questioned the success of my marriage to Mack he never expressed that to me. He was basically letting me make my own bed and I would have to lie in it.

I did not feel safe in Mack's town and I felt that I did not belong. I was too outspoken, too impulsive, and too opinionated to fit into his world. I did not know how to turn my personality off to accommodate the judgment of others so that I might better fit into this small town. Religious zealots and community icons that placed themselves above everyone else surrounded me, and I did not know how to adapt to these pretentious standards. The demeanor this community required of me just wasn't me!

"Mack" I cried out to him many nights, "I am dying here! You have got to get me out of this town. I can't explain it, but I can feel it!"
"You are being foolish!" he responded, "There is nothing wrong with you."
"I hate it here. I feel like I have to pretend to be someone I'm not! Please Mack let's move somewhere else, please!" I wailed at him time and time again as tears streamed down my cheeks.
Mack simply discounted my feelings and rolled over and went to sleep. Nothing ever changed.

Mack and I went to eat at a local restaurant and pub for drinks and dinner, but before we could enter we had to be sure that none of his church mongers were lurking about and learn that we were entering a bar. Once inside we sat down and were joined by a local physician who was anything but a stuffy religious zealot. In this man's company I actually began to relax and enjoy myself. The doctor was Catholic and had a pack of kids. Among the local gossipers it was reported that he was a bit of a playboy. I felt at ease with him. Of course I would because he was more like me. The doctor and I were joking around about the Pope and birth control.

"My Mother always said that the rhythm method doesn't work, because she has five living examples," I laughingly said to the doctor.
"Yea me too" He said
"She said that every time she took off her bobby socks, she got pregnant"
We all laughed and the doctor asked, "Why do I have so many kids then, I don't even wear bobby socks."
"Maybe it's what you didn't wear." I said with a smirk on my face, implying that a condom might have been in order.

Through the Eyes of Betsy McCall

Right at that moment I felt a kick on my shin under the table and I looked at Mack who was telling me to shut up with his eyes.
The doctor responded that he'd take the kid rather than wrap it.
I simply smiled at him and did not respond with a come back. Mack had reprimanded me and I knew it was time to stop being myself again and go back to the image that he was forcing me to grow into.

This happened to me too many times in different settings because I was too out spoken and too outgoing and this was not conducive to the Hunsdorfer image. Mack was always shooting me down and telling me to be quiet and eventually he got his way. Over time I became the *'Stepford Wife' that he wanted.

By the time Gabrielle was born, I would not leave the house without looking like I had just walked off of the pages of Vogue magazine. I would not even go to the mailbox without make up applied. When Gabrielle was conceived and I shared this news with Uncle Howard he replied, "How did you get pregnant, didn't you have to mess up your hair?"
That may seem like a sarcastic thing for him to say but it was true, and he knew it. I had become obsessed with trying to achieve perfection and never saying or doing the wrong thing in front of the wrong people.

I was living a lie just as all the hypocritical Hornsdorfers were. They were chameleons and they changed their skin according to the company they kept. In time I learned to change my skin too; in fact I destroyed my original self in order to fit into this new world. I did not want to do anything to bring shame to Aunt Elise as my grandfather had requested.

It seemed that Mack and I could go nowhere or do anything without the companionship of his parents or at the very least his mother when his father was away on business. Now married Mack and I could no longer go out for dinner alone, go to the lake and boat or even go to church on Sunday without being accompanied by his parents or the entourage of his entire family. As inseparable as they were as a family, church on Sunday morning was bizarre. His parents would take their car Tony would take his car,

*1

C. R. Perk

Paula would take her car and when Skye was old enough to drive he took his car. There would be a total of four cars at the church to transport five people from home to church and back. Every Sunday after church Mack and I joined the entire family for dinner at the big house. It seemed that Mack and I could not consume food on Sunday with out the presence of his family, but the unity of the family seemed as if they had to force continuity.

Some years into the marriage I took a composition class at the junior college in my hometown. It was only one night a week but it gave me motivation to write again. In that class I wrote the following paper about a setting at the dinner table with this family.
My instructor had wanted to keep the paper, but I was not willing to leave my dirty laundry for him to use in future class settings.

Grandpa's Success

The dining room was warm and inviting, filled with mouth-watering aromas of roast beef, hot muffins and freshly brewed coffee. However there was an absence of continuity, and a subtle trace of tension in the room. Those present spoke to one another but there seemed to be a lack of true communication.

"A, B, C, D..." the two year old recited for her grandfather. Her tiny voice sang sweetly above the clatter of dishware and the tinkling of ice in glasses as the family ate their Sunday dinner.

"X, Y, Z!" she proudly finished as she smiled up at her grandfather with expectations of praise.

"That's pretty good," he said, "except that you forgot the letter M."

He was always the perfectionist, capitalizing on weakness and over looking accomplishment. Of course near perfection wouldn't be good enough, even if she were only a toddler.

"Did you know," his wife asked, "that the Cassidy's baby was born breach?"

At that moment he looked away from her to his son and asked. "How are sales down at the plant?"

Everything was always business! Before husbandry, fatherhood or persona, he was always a businessman. Money, success, position, power and material things that money could buy were his gratifications in life.

As he passed the meat platter, the custom made initial ring he always wore glittered in the light. The letters were formed by inlaid diamonds and were the same formation of the logo on his company letterhead.

He was very successful in his business, and his family enjoyed the financial benefits. They wanted nothing in the material sense, but he never let them forget how hard he had worked for those provisions.

"Hey dad," his son asked, "how about nine holes of golf this afternoon?"
"I don't have time for play now son. I really wish that I did." He responded implying that his son should be indebted to him for having frivolous playtime.
"Someday," he continued, "I plan on relaxing too, but today Joe and I have to fly out to L.A."

As his wife cleared the table, he prepared to leave. He kissed his granddaughter goodbye, and then impatiently stood jiggling his car keys with his hands in his pockets.

He looked handsome standing there in his impeccably tailored suit. His physique still looked youthful despite his fifty years. He still had a full head of blonde hair and his mustache seemed to take years off of his face. The years had been kind to him.

After he dutifully kissed his wife and said goodbye to his family, he drove his imported Mercedez Benz to the airport where the Lear was hangered.

Mack's father once said to me, "Mack has some pretty big feet, but he can't fill his old man's shoes."
Others were quoted as saying that Elias Hunsdorfer was not a brilliant businessman but his secretary Janice was. He paid her well and she may well have been the brains that governed his success. Whatever the circumstances of his success, he had prepared Mack for nothing and I became the victim of a mental delusion, admittedly my own mistake.

When I became pregnant and carried Gabrielle, I did not gain body weight due to fat cells, but I blew up like a blimp. I retained water everywhere including my face, feet and hands. I walked past one of my best friends from high school when shopping at the mall and she did not even recognize me because my face was so engorged with fluid. By some miracle I never became toxic. The opinion that women are their most beautiful during pregnancy did not apply to me. I looked absolutely horrible! When I gave birth to her I weighed a whopping 180 pounds, and three days later when we left the hospital I had urinated 60 pounds of water out of my body and except for a little loose skin I was back to my before conception weight. The same scenario occurred through my pregnancy with Seth, and no one could believe that I could get back to pre-pregnancy weight in less than five days, especially since I had looked like the *Hindenburg* the week before.

My children brought me great joy and satisfaction. I now had something to occupy my time. They kept me busy and I rejoiced in caring for them. However the children did not resolve the problems between Mack and I but neither did they make it any worse. Our children served to cement the illusion that we were the perfect family and I had long ago learned how to play the part.

Following the birth of our children Mack and I maintained a sexual relationship, but each and every time we had intercourse I became nauseated following the intimacy. I did not understand this and neither did Mack, but once it started it never stopped.

In the following years I developed gastro-intestinal pain that I thought I would die from.
I went to our family physician and he ordered a complete GI series and nothing was found. There was nothing wrong with my digestive system.
While suffering one of these episodes in the company of Uncle Howard he said to me, and I quote, "You just need to fart."
If it were that simple I would have been creating wind all over the place, but I couldn't.
I think there may have been some truth to his advice, but I was unable to pass gas because it was not becoming to my image.

Then the headaches began and I suffered from sinus infections that settled in my chest and made me cough like I was chronically ill. This was followed by a series of allergy tests where I learned that I was sensitive to everything from yeast to dog hair and dander.

I was given a series of injections to combat the reactions to these allergens that had little effect, and eventually I had sinus surgery in an effort to create better drainage. The surgery was unnecessary because my sinuses were not packed with mucus.

I was young, beautiful and healthy as a horse. My body was well it was my mind that was not.

Mack's ability to stop providing for his mother never happened. She called and Mack jumped. I recall one night when a dark storm was approaching and there were tornado warnings out for our area. Mack's mother called and asked him to come to the big house to tie down the plane and secure the hanger doors.
"I'll be right there." He had said into the phone.
"Where are you going now?" I asked.
"Mom needs me to go out to tie down the plane and secure the hanger doors." Mack replied.
"Why in the hell is it always you?" I angrily asked him, "There are two other boys out there that are perfectly capable of doing that. Why can't Skye or Tony do it?"
"She has more confidence in me and I have always taken care of things when dad wasn't around." He replied.
"So with a terrible storm coming, you have to leave your family to go take care of your mother, and leave us here to ride this out by ourselves?" I asked him my voice rising to another octave.
"I have to go." He flatly stated and out the door he went.
Mack and I never argued, but whenever there was an issue between us he always reacted the same way. Ignore it, it will go away and eventually it always did.

I think it was that night that I finally realized that Mack had never been weaned from his mother and no matter how old he grew to be he never would be. Mack was paralyzed by his family and I had not married a man, I had married a man and his mother. Mack's relationship to his mother went somewhere beyond normal bonding and this occurred because of his fathers constant absence throughout Mack's entire childhood.

C. R. Perk

It was ironic that the very thing that I had denied myself was Mack's greatest weakness.

I grew to resent his mother on a level that I cannot even fathom to put into words. She was dependant upon my husband and she came first no matter what I wanted or needed. I had needed to get out this town years ago, but that could not possibly have happened because that would have caused Mack to have to be weaned. Mack I came to realize could only co-exist with his mother. My rock of Gibraltar had turned out to be a simpering wimp that could do nothing on his own. He needed his father for employment and his mother for nurturing. I did not understand and it drove me nuts. I had wanted my entire life to go somewhere and accomplish great things with the man that I loved. I had fully expected Mack to want the same things out of our life together. Of course I never spoke of it before the marriage; I simply assumed that it would happen that way.

I never disputed Mack's decisions or choices. If Mack wanted a Monte Carlo we bought a Monte Carlo, if Mack wanted scratch and dent furniture we purchased scratch and dent furniture. So when Mack decided to purchase a newly constructed duplex, we bought the duplex. In order to purchase the property Mack borrowed the down payment from his Amish grandfather. Mack's grandfather was one of the kindest men I have ever met and I had enormous respect for him, but his life style and mine never even got close to one another. I possess not one drop of Dutch blood. My heritage is Irish Catholic with a splash of Cherokee. Mack's Amish grandfather was born on July 4th, 1900. To honor his birthday, we had to go to the Amish farmhouse every year on the 4th and it did not matter what else might be planned for the holiday; we had to go to the farm for an Amish birthday celebration. This was one of the most maddening things I have ever endured in my life. Every female in the house with the exceptions of infants and toddlers were in the kitchen preparing fish, rice, dressing and an assortment of other starchy dishes, while every male present sat in the living area discussing the weather, farming and finance. The Amish have truly not progressed one iota in the past one hundred and fifty years, and the sexual segregation and discrimination made me want to scream. I already had a bad attitude because I had just left a pool party or a cook out to come all the way out here to become a slave to a propane stove, a sink full of dishwater and about forty dirty plates. An Amish birthday was not my idea of a Fourth of

July celebration. Of course this was made even more pleasant by the fact that we were forbidden to smoke or drink on the property and the beverage selection was well water without ice.

I went because I never defied Mack and also because I did not want to hurt the old man's feelings by refusing to attend to his birthday celebration. Mack would never have been absent and my absence would have caused all kinds of embarrassment. So being the obedient android that I had become, I went every year and every year I hated it more than the year before.

I learned two things from Mack's Amish heritage: women belong in the kitchen barefoot and pregnant, (literally, they never wore shoes and they had no other means of recreation in the evening than to make babies, lots of babies!), and how to make stuffing that is to die for.

In ten years I have not one memory of an enjoyable gathering with Mack's extended relatives. They were always the same, always boring and I was always forced to make simplistic small talk with a bunch of people that I felt were judgmental, pretentious, and had nothing in common with me. To add insult to injury, the sexual segregation was always present no matter where the gathering occurred.

This is not to say that these people were not good, caring, kind, and God fearing people. Most of them had actually left the Amish life style and were now practicing Mennonites.

Still the progression from the practice that worldly was a sin to a more contemporary lifestyle, did little to change their demeanor and they still had too much of the old Dutch in them for me. These people were just simply made of a far different fiber than me.

In short, I hated being married to Mack and his family. He should have left the outspoken blonde in the bar that fateful night and gone home to find himself a nice little Mennonite girl.

Chapter 15

After six years in the Navy, Royce finally came home. He had gifts for everyone from all over the world and he brought me a real cameo broach from Italy. Although I abhor the practice of killing elephants for their tusks, I could not give the elephant its tusk back or its life. I loved the broach and the sentiment with which it was given. I still have that broach to this day.

Royce came to my home to visit and present his gift and soon after his arrival he decided that we needed to go into town to get some beer. I had not been out of the duplex so I had not spent my hour in front of the mirror.
"Hold on," I said, "I have to clean up before we go."
Off I went to apply my make up, perfect my hair and put on appropriate clothes.
"You don't have to do all of that to go into town to get beer," Royce had complained.
"Yes I do," I said and no amount of cajoling from Royce could alter my quest to achieve my perfect public image.
"What has happened to you?" Royce questioned, "You were never like this before."
"Nothing has happened to me, I just don't go out without looking my best." I responded.
The truth was that I had become obsessed with my appearance in public and I could not overcome it.

I later learned that Royce asked Donna, Uncle Howard and Ellie what had happened to me since he left. They all had witnessed the changes gradually and did not know what to tell him.
Ellie did offer this much to satisfy his curiosity, "She has changed and Joe won't even go up to see her with me because her house looks like a furniture store display room and he's is afraid to move in that apartment. She is also very critical of my house keeping skills and it pisses Joe off. It's really kind of sad because they used to be so close."

"She does keep an unbelievably clean house," Royce responded. "If she uses a coffee cup she has to wash it and put it away immediately. If she uses the ashtray she empties it and wipes it out before she uses it the next time and when Gabrielle got some toys out to play with, she went back to the toy closet for something else and came back to tell her mom not to put her toys away because she was playing with them. Charlie must pick up the kids toys before she even has a chance to play with them."

Still Royce was the only one that was really concerned about me and not enough so to pursue it any further. I had become obsessive about my looks and my house keeping but that hardly constituted a mental disorder.

What it constituted was a need to control. I had lost control of my life and the only way I could cope was total control of my environment, my appearance and my children.

Gabrielle retaliated to the control by misbehaving. She liked to pull all of the LPs out of their jackets and throw them all over the living room floor. If that did not get my immediate attention then she would go get baby powder from her changing table and powder the tops of my coffee and end tables, then rub her hands all over the tops of them.

I was unable to potty train Gabrielle until she was three years old because she refused to use the potty chair. She was telling me without the capacity to say the words that I could control everything else that she did but not her body functions. It took her spending time with another child her age for her to make the decision to control her toilet habits. Just when Gabrielle decided it was time to potty in the toilet I learned that I was pregnant again.

Seth was born the following October two and a half weeks late. His entire berthing process was an hour and forty- five minutes. It was as if he had finally decided to come out and he didn't want to waste time doing it. He weighed in at a healthy nine pounds two ounces, smoking a cigar and wanted to know where the poker game was. He raised his head in the hospital nursery. I could not believe this child was related to his sister. He was the ugliest infant I have ever seen but time was kind and he became model material as an adorable toddler.

Soon after the berth of Seth, Mack, both children, and myself loaded up into the car and headed to Sarasota, Florida once more. For the entire duration of our marriage with the exception of a trip to Nashville this was our vacation destination every year. This trip however was for our participation in Paula's wedding.

Paula was about to marry a handsome young attorney that had an ego the size of Texas. His name was Patrick, and he had done well for himself. Paula had gotten her masters in Nursing so their future was pretty secure.

Quite by accident, Patrick had come over to admire my new son as I nursed him and he got a glimpse of my rather large engorged breast. He tactfully retreated and apologized through this embarrassing moment but the image must have haunted him.

In the days before the wedding the enormous wedding party was hanging out and partying together. At this time it was legal for people to drink and be mobile in Florida as long as the driver was not consuming alcohol. Patrick and Paula had rented a bus to take the entire wedding party out to party and the company that they rented the bus from provided a driver.

We were all really having a good time. This was completely different than any of the images that were maintained in our northern existence. We hopped from bar to bar to bar with coolers overflowing on the bus. Everyone was drinking and having a great time. I went to the bathroom in the back of the bus and as I attempted to leave Patrick came into the miniscule cubicle. He wanted to see my breasts.
"You are marrying my sister in law in two days, what do you think you are doing?" I asked him through my astonishment.
"Oh come on," He said, "I just want to touch them. Let me feel them, Paula doesn't have big breast like you."
"Patrick you are drunk and stupid. Get away from me." I had rebelled.
"Come on," he said, "just one little feel. I'm getting married and I won't have this chance again." He persisted as he attempted to get inside my blouse.
"Patrick, I am married! To your fiancé's brother! Now get away from me!" I flatly stated as I shoved past him to get out of that bathroom.

I was extremely upset by this blatant lack of respect for me, my husband and above all his future wife! My fun was now over for the evening.

I actually told Mack what had occurred. Mack responded to this as he did all situations that he did not want to deal with. He said and did nothing. Once again I felt that I was a secondary priority in Mack's life.

The wedding was spectacular, with a sit down meal complete with ice carvings. This reception was to accommodate the Amish that were present and then a second reception that the Amish knew nothing about was held in a large ballroom at an area motel. As the reception ball room filled with guests and the band warmed up, the wedding party was pairing up for our intros. We entered the ballroom under a spotlight one pair at a time and began to dance as our names were bellowed through the microphone. Finally the entire wedding party was on the floor and the bride and groom were introduced as Mr. and Mrs. Patrick Bittle.

It was the classiest wedding I have ever witnessed and certainly ever been a participant of. It must to have cost Elias Hunsdorfer a minimum of twenty thousand dollars.

We returned to our home in Illinois, and resumed our lives as before and nothing was ever said about Patrick's misconduct.

A year later I went to my hometown to do some Christmas shopping and meet up with my old friend Toni for drinks. After rushing through my shopping I met Toni at a local pub and to my astonishment, she was not alone. Sitting there on a bar stool beside her was none other than Kodie.

"Oh my God!" I ranted, "I can't believe that you are here. How are you?"
"I'm good, and I'm really here in the flesh." He responded grinning.
Toni had set this up and I knew it but I could have cared less, I was so excited to see him again.
"Don't I look, OK?" he asked.
"You look wonderful." I responded.

He had put on about 30 pounds but he wasn't overweight, he was simply larger and solid as a concrete wall. He was as handsome as I'd remembered him and still just as arrogant. Not everyone shared my opinion of his good looks, but he was still handsome to me, and he was still the person that I had fallen in love with twelve years earlier.

I was so excited that I could hardly contain it. I wasn't in Mack's town now, I was in mine and I felt the freedom come rushing into my heart as if it were a fresh burst of air. I would have sworn that the hole in my heart had stopped its lonely howl as the emptiness faded away. I was sitting next to Kodie again and that was all that mattered to me at that moment,

We started with small talk as we got reacquainted and drank our beers.
"How many kids do you have now?" he asked me.
"I have two, Gabrielle is four and Seth is fourteen months, how about you?"
I heard him talking but I didn't hear him say how many children he had because I really didn't care. My heart was full and I was basking in his presence.

We continued to drink beer and share small talk before the alcohol took affect and we loosened up.
"Where do you work, what do you drive, where do you live, what have been doing with yourself, are you happy," that type of conversation and then he suddenly changed the path of everything.

"I could not believe that you had an abortion." He said. "Do you know what that did to me? You didn't even ask me if I wanted you to do that."
"I know I'm sorry, but the decision was taken out of my hands. I had wanted to go away, give berth and put the child up for adoption but Aunt Elise would not stand for it."
"Oh ya," he laughed, "the woman that so loved me."
"Ya her," I said as I grinned at him.
"Did she know that I was the Father?" he asked.
"Yes, but when I told her your name she did not make the connection right away." I replied.
"What connection?" he asked.

"That you were the molester." I said with a bit of accusation and mirth in my voice.
"Oh that. I can't believe that you even told her about that." He replied with a bit of indignation in his voice.
"It was the only way I could save my own ass." I laughed. "I had to tell her, I was very upset by that incident."
"Ya, I should not have done that to you. I was a stupid punk kid and I really thought you would play." He replied somewhat apologetically.
"It's over Kodie, we're not kids anymore." I responded, "I forgave you a long time ago. Of course Aunt Elise never did. She never forgave you and she never forgot."
"Nothin to be done about it now." He said with a smirk on his face.

We continued to talk and reminisce about old times and good times. The more we drank, the more familiar we became. He placed his hand on my leg and I did not stop him, in fact I enjoyed it. He put his arm around my back and I hungrily leaned into his massive chest and laid my head on his shoulder. I was delirious in his presence and I think he felt it too.

At the close of the evening we went to his car to escape the bitter cold elements outdoors, and it was then that he leaned over to kiss me and he did not stop kissing me. I sat in that car for a very long time and we necked as if we were teenagers again. My heart was singing and I did not want this night to end.

"Are we going to see one another again?" I asked him almost pleading.
"We're both married now Charlie. I think we really shouldn't." he replied.

I could not argue that point but I didn't have to leave yet either. I stayed in that car drinking up his kisses until he finally said, "I really have to go."
"I know I do to." I replied.
So after one last lingering kiss, I got out of his car and went to mine. I drove the thirty miles back to Fredericks without remorse and said not a word to Mack about what had occurred.

On that fateful night the 'Stepford Wife' of Mack Hunsdorfer died and Charletta Raye was reborn.

C. R. Perk

Chapter 16

When I awoke the following morning, nothing was the same. I was consumed by anxiety. An unexplained fear that seemed to have no justification and came from nothing I could grasp. It was horrible and I felt frightened all of the time. This lasted for weeks and the fear was coupled by thoughts of Kodie. I could not get him out of my thoughts. It seemed that I could not go on living without him. He was the link in my mind to my very survival and happiness.

I was obsessed with seeing him again and I didn't understand it. My every breath carried his name, and I was consumed with the thought of those kisses. My unknown fear was so strong that I could not eat and I felt I wanted to vomit when I tried.
I had only kissed him. Deeply and passionately true but I didn't commit adultery. Why was I experiencing this horrid fear of something unknown?
In fact why would I want him at all, he was to my minds thinking beneath me now.
I was the wife of Mack Hunsdorfer, I had two beautiful children and a stable home, why would I want a 4 X 4 truck driver over Mack? None of this made any sense.

But no matter how I tried to reason the situation, I always came back to the same conclusion. I was in love with Kodie and I could not bear not having him!

In less than a month I had lost ten pounds that I could not afford to lose. Clinically I had become anorexic. My life was emotionally out of control now and I had found yet another way to control. My fingernails became grooved due to the lack of nutrition, and I stopped menstruating. Then suddenly I began to spot daily.
I went to my family physician (the same that had ordered the G.I. series) and he felt a grapefruit sized cyst on my right ovary.

I went to my gynecologist who found nothing, but she did see the madness in my eyes. The cyst had burst before I got to her office but the cyst was not the problem and it was probably induced due to the stress and anxiety.
The gynecologist spoke to Uncle Howard and told him, despite patient privacy, that I was not well emotionally, psychologically, or perhaps both.

The madness continued and my obsession did not subside. I tried to find ways to accidentally run into Kodie. I went back to the pub where we had met before but he was never there. I stood on street corners waiting and watching for his truck to be making deliveries in Fredericks. I frequently saw the truck but he never stopped to speak to me. I even went to the local country club in hopes of seeing him deliver there, and again I never was able to accidentally be in the right place at the right time. I think he was on a mission to avoid me at all cost.
He was making the only intelligent decision he could make. Whether he had any of the same feelings for me or not, he was married with a family and he was not prepared to disrupt that. Quite honesty, I doubt that I would have been strong enough to do anything more than sneak away with him myself. I could not have left Mack at that time, no matter how much I thought that I could.

It became obvious that Kodie was avoiding me, so that made the obsession all the greater. I had always wanted what I could not have and I was clearly not what he wanted.
Still the big question remained, 'why did I want him?'
I had the all American dream and I wanted to throw it all away for a lowly beer truck driver. This made absolutely no sense at all!!!!!

When I could no longer bear the anxiety, the anorexia, or the mental anguish, I went to the telephone directory and called the Mental Health Center and made an appointment to see a psychologist. It takes a lot of pain to push any individual to go to that extreme.

I entered the dreary old building that had twelve- foot tall windows in the store- front, mini blinds and olive green paint on the walls. It was not a show place and was not equipped to be anything more than what it was. A place for lost hearts to go to try to find their peace, and here I was.

I nervously sat alone in my Vogue image with my perfectly manicured nails, (except for the grooves), and waited for someone to come summons me.

She was tall, blonde, blue eyed, very young and pretty in a simple plain way.
She came to me and motioned for me to follow her through the door to a small room equipped with several chairs, a small table and a lamp.
I entered the sparsely furnished room and she told me to sit in one of the chairs.
She took another chair beside the table.
"My name is Angel," she said to me.
"My name is Charlie," I said to the unasked question.
She simply looked at me and waited for me to speak.
"This is hard," I said to her.
She simply nodded and waited for me to continue.
Then I blurted out to her, "My life is nuts."
"What's going on?" she asked me.
"I am married to a handsome successful man, we have two beautiful children, a nice home, the all American dream and I am obsessed with this nobody beer truck driver from my past." I stated.
"Why am I having these feelings?" I pleaded to her.
Angel, as any good therapist did not offer any answers only more questions.
Her questions were none stop. It takes a very long time for a therapist to obtain enough information to assist a client and in the following months, Angel learned more about me than I knew myself.

We began our weekly chats discussing my obsession but she prompted me for deeper information.
"What is going on with you and Mack?" she had asked me.
"Nothing really," I responded. "I don't want to be with him anymore, I think we are sexually incompatible...."
Angel did not coddle that theory and she prompted me for yet more information.

One small stone turned over after another, and so our sessions went for many months. Angel was prompting me for information that I was slowly feeding back to her. All the while she was documenting meaningful information.

It took many months before my obsession changed from Kodie and my miserable marriage, to understanding my own neurosis. Angel's questions prompted me to go backwards in time and challenged me to deal with feelings long since forgotten. Her gentle questions prompted me to go to the source of my neurosis, and deal with the reality of why I was there
Over many months we discussed my childhood and my separation from my mother.
"Do not under estimate the impact that your separation from your mother had on you." She had advised me.

Soon after she spoke those words, she had two chairs facing one another when I arrived for our session.
"I want you to sit in this chair, and the one that is facing you I want you to pretend that your mother is sitting in it. I want you to talk to that chair as if you were speaking to your mother and I want you to tell your mother how you feel." said Angel.
Oh my God, I was not prepared for this. Nothing could have prepared me for this!
It felt awkward and embarrassed to speak to an empty chair.
I sat in the selected chair and faced the empty one as Angel prompted the questions.
"Tell your Mother how you felt when she never came for you." She said.
"I was hurt and lonely and I felt like you didn't love me." I said as tears brimmed in my eyelids.
"Tell her why you felt that way." Angel prompted.
I was holding my arms across my chest and rocking back and forth, as if to shelter myself from the pain.
"Because I felt like I was not worth you taking any interests in me. I felt like I was nothing!" I wailed through my tears.
I was amazed at how quickly Angel had hit the tender spots that she was targeting and more surprised by how swiftly I had responded to those feelings.

"Tell your mother what you wish she had done to make you not feel these things." Again she prompted me.

Now rocking harder and feeling the full impact of this session I began to lose control, my tears were uncontrollable and my voice was breaking up as I responded, "I wanted you to come for me, I wanted you to confront Aunt Elise and Uncle Howard, and I wanted you to care enough that you would show up on our doorstep. I wanted you show me something that said I was worth your love, but you never did!" I said as I crumpled into a heap of tears.

"That's enough," Angel said, "take a break."

I spoke to Uncle Howard and told him that I was being counseled which he thought was a very good idea. He did forewarn me however that I would get much worse before I got better. Truer words have never been spoken.

My new obsession now was to understand my neurosis and the full impact of my feelings of abandonment. Angel gave me a book titled *"Your Inner Child of the Past', and it became my bible. I learned in this book that almost all of my activities and choices over the years could have been predicted. I was the classic child of abandonment, complete with sexual misconduct, no conscience about those activities, and ultimately self-esteem that is virtually non-existent.

"Charlie," Angel said to me one day, "I recognize that in order for you to give yourself permission to feel something, you have to first understand it. That's why I gave you that book. Now I'm going to tell you something else. There are a lot of people out there that do not have the intelligence to understand this, but you do. You are extremely intelligent and you can do this, I promise you."

On that day Angel had given me the greatest gift of all. I was not only, not stupid, but I was smart!

During my therapy sessions with Angel, I received a call from my mother who said that she had developed a nagging cough.

*3

"Do you feel ill?" I asked her.
"No," she said. "I feel fine, except for this G-damn cough"
"Mom, this sounds like cancer, you need to go to the doctor now!" I responded.
"I have an appointment to see the doctor in about six weeks. I'll talk to him about it then." My mother responded
"Mom, you need to call him now." I reiterated.
But there was nothing I could say to make her change her appointment time.
I hung up the phone and I was very upset. At first I said nothing to Mack but I was getting a glass of milk for Gabrielle and I dropped the gallon of milk on the floor. I just slid down the counter and sat on the floor and began to cry,
"What is wrong?" Mack asked me as I buried my tear-streaked face into my hands.
I was crying hysterically and all of a sudden I looked up at Mack and began to laugh just as hysterically. "Do you realize that I am crying over spilled milk?"
Of course it had nothing to do with milk.
Now my mother who had never mothered me was probably going to die from cancer!

Then suddenly everything took a turn when Mack's parents having lost their fortune suddenly decided to move to Florida. It was then decided that Mack and I should move into the big house in the country. I had grave reservations about that. I spoke to Angel about it at length and she knew the contempt that I felt for Mack's parents. Angel offered no advice but tried to talk me through an intelligent decision. It would have made no difference whether I wanted to move out there or not, it never did, so we packed up and left the duplex to move to the big house in the country. We rented the other side of the duplex out to the single man that I eventually evicted when Mack stole the children.

In truth I liked living out there once we moved and his parents were out of the state. I enjoyed the privacy and the amenities. However his mother had to come home to visit and while I had made some changes to the house and furnishings it was still her house. She drove me to near distraction when she came. I love sunlight and I would open all the drapes and mini blinds in the house. I would no more than leave the room and she would close them all. I didn't care how big this house was it was not big enough for two queen bees.

It angered her that I would not put my children down for naps and go out to mow the landing strip. The mower moved at about 5 mph and I was not willing to be three acres away while my children slept. Anything could happen I retaliated.

"Well I did it all the time when my kids were small." She had argued.

"That was you, not me. If the house caught on fire or God knows what could happen, I couldn't get here quick enough. I will not do it!" I responded and on this issue I would not budge.

Thank the Lord for Angel, if no one else wanted to listen to me complain she always listened intently to all of my whining, but she always pulled me back to things that I needed to deal with.

I shared with her that Boyd had also moved his family to Florida and that I had recently sent him a letter and he did not respond to it. I was so upset that I sent him another letter and told him that he had pissed me off. He rudely wrote on the second letter that it was better to be pissed off than pissed on and sent it back to me. I was very upset by that.

"What were you feeling when you got that letter back?" Angel asked me.

"I was more pissed!" I said.

"No you weren't" she replied, "Anger is always a secondary reaction to something else. We use it to protect ourselves. What were you really feeling?"

"I guess it hurt my feelings," I said.

She nodded her head and asked, "Anything else?"

"Yea, he just has shut himself off from us since he moved to Florida and I don't understand." I confessed.

"So how do you feel about him shutting you out?" she asked me.

"It hurts my feelings, I miss him terribly and he wants to crawl up into a cocoon." I replied.

"What else do you feel Charlie, come on you can say the words," she prompted me.

"He left me, and that hurts." I said as tears welled up in my eyes once more.
"Don't you mean that he abandoned you too?" she asked me.
"Yes," I said as the tears just kept coming.

I beat the steering wheel of my car all the way home and I cussed Boyd as I had never cussed anyone in my life. He had abandoned me too but even worse he had shut me out of his life.

At some point during my counseling with Angel I took my "bible" to Mack, and I shared with him what I had learned through my counseling. I also encouraged him to find his 'Inner Child of the Past', which of course he never did. He was an almighty Hunsdorder, and far too high above these neurosis that have and still do plague generations of people.
I did however tell him that I could not believe that my mother had just accepted that I was no longer an active participant in her life.
"If someone took my kids from me, I don't care where they were, I would walk to get them back if I had to." I had said to Mack.
To which the lying bastard responded, "I would never take our kids from you."

Then after two years of sharing my deepest and darkest secrets with Angel, she said she had something very important to talk with me about.

We sat in our usual chairs and I looked at her as I waited for her to continue.
"This is going to be very hard for both of us," she said.
I looked at her and waited for what ever it was that she was about to share with me.
"My husband has been offered a very good job in Connecticut and we are going to move very soon," she said.
I just buried my face in my hands and started to cry uncontrollably.
Angel's eyes filled with tears and she said, "This is hard for me too. I have grown very fond of you and I will miss you."
I just looked at her through my tears. I had grown to trust Angel more than I had trusted anyone in my life. She was indeed my 'angel 'and she had

helped me through so much. She had given my self back to me. I could not conceive how I would manage without her guidance and compassion.

Angel continued, "I know how badly this hurts you. Once again you are feeling abandoned, and I am saddened that we have to part this way, but I know that you are well enough to go forward with your life now and you don't really need me anymore."

"Yes I do!, I managed to choke out. "I do still need you."

Through her tears Angle said, "No you really don't you are only frightened to make the break from me."

Angel had counseled me for two years, she had pulled things from my soul and understood them. No one had ever understood those thoughts and feelings. Perhaps she had filled the role of a maternal figure that cared unconditionally for my feelings. Angel had become the very best friend that I had ever had in my life and she knew more than anyone did or ever would again.

As tears streamed down both of our faces I asked her, "What will I do with out you?"

"You will go on with your life. You will still have to fight the demons from time to time, but now you know how to fight them. You are stronger now and better informed about what torments you, and you will be fine." Angel said in conclusion.

She gave me the name of another counselor in a larger city and advised me to contact her to participate in group counseling.

At the close of that day's session, Angel gave me an enormous hug. I knew then that she loved me as much as I had grown to love her. We said our good-byes and I cried all the way home. I never saw Angel again, but I did receive a birth announcement some months later. I had never even known that she was pregnant.

Chapter 17

At the close of my therapy sessions with Angel, I did attend group counseling. For all that it was supposed to benefit me it only served to reinforce my previous behavior. I met with a group of women who were equally neurotic and shared with the group their experiences with adultery and abuse. In a way it gave me permission to continue to eroticize my feelings. The old verbiage, 'birds of feather flock together', certainly applied in these settings. They were nice women; they were simply as much or more screwed up than I had been.
I was much stronger after my counseling, but I was not 100% and I was prone to relapses of previous misconducts.
Thus a brief affair with a married man 20 years my senior did nothing to promote my mental health. Following the brief unsatisfying affair, I decided to go to work.

Mack and I had been members at the local country club for several years. Mack had joined for the golf benefits and I was a tag along at times, but for the most part left at home. I had complained to Mack that he was never home. One night a week he met with the Lions club, another week night he played poker with the guys, another night of the week he was bowling on a league, and another night of the week he played golf on the men's golf league at the country club, so when the chairwoman of the ladies golf league telephoned me and asked if I wanted to join the league, I said. "Hell yes!"
So Mack and I went and purchased clubs, a bag, balls, tees, shoes, etc. and I started playing golf. At first we went to the driving range where I doffed the ball repeatedly and then all of a sudden I made contact and sent the ball sailing! Once I got the feel for my swing, I was hooked. I never became the best golfer on the ladies league, but I definitely hit the longest ball. These are the only memorable and pleasant memories I have with Mack. We both became avid golfers and as a team we were serious adversaries to our opponents.

We were once in sudden death playoff in a couple's tournament and we were on the eighteenth hole, but it was really the 27th hole as we were circling again in the elimination process. It was Mack and me and another couple for the championship. On this hole the woman's tee gave us a great advantage for me to take the tee shot. One of Mack's friends said to Mack, "Why are you letting her tee? This is a par five." Seconds later I drove the tee shot 270 yards down the fairway, and Mack turned to his friend and said, "That's why."

Mack took the second shot and laid the ball near the green, I chipped it close and Mack putted it in for a birdie. We won the tournament. Our days on the golf course were wonderful and I had found a place that I felt more accepted. We always went to the nineteenth hole to socialize and I found the patrons there to be much more to my liking.

So it should have come as no surprise to Mack that when I decided to go to work that I should choose to go to the country club where I asked for the bartender's position.

The managers of the club were thrilled to have me come on board and could not believe their good fortune in getting a pretty lady with knowledge about the game. I enjoyed the game and the job so it was a wonderful solution for all of us.

I quickly learned how to pour vodka and gin martini's, Early Times, Southern Comfort, and open a lot of beers. I fit in well and was truly having a very good time.

Everyone was happy, the golfing bar patrons, the managers, and me! So why did Mack have to be so adamantly opposed to me taking this position? Because it was unbecoming a Hunsdorfer of course! I was stronger now though and I refused to back down to his demands this time. I took the job and I enjoyed the job for a short time. I could throw drinks and handle the bar when it was packed. I did it well and I was rewarded with hefty tips. I opened my own checking account and bought my own used car. This was the first car that I had ever personally owned. I was in pursuit of my own happiness and finding my sense of self worth. I had stepped out of the *'Stepford Wife' image and was doing what I wanted to do for a change.

*2

While I was tending bar, the cook was preparing food for the patrons. Every night after the kitchen closed, the cook would come to the bar for a beer. He had gold eyes, somewhere between brown and yellow, and he studied people with them. He was always looking at people suspiciously and shooting his eyes around the room. I found him to be fascinating and when I began to make conversation with him he was mysterious and did not reveal a lot about himself. That intrigued me even more. So of course it became my mission to find out what was lurking behind those cold gold eyes.

I struck up conversation with him and learned that he was single, five years younger than me, and had a job in a factory during the day and then came to work in the evening to cook at the country club. This seemed to be commendable. He also had a passion for golf, for drinking and eventually for me. He would bring me something from the kitchen each evening and later confessed that he had put extra care into my meals. He drove a piece of junk Chevrolet that was so rusted out that you could see the road beneath the floor board, and he dressed like a bum. But I was still fascinated.

His name was Jay and he represented something irresponsible and playful. I was attracted to him on the bases of friendship at first, but as his flirtations became more advanced so did my perception of how I thought about him. It wasn't long before we were drinking together in the club in the evening. The manager had a drinking problem and he loved having company, so after most of the crowd had left we would all sit together, drink for free and socialize. It was during these late hours that I got to know Jay better. Perhaps better than I should have.

It was May, and Mothers Day was approaching. I told Jay that I would be at the club for a Mothers Day celebration.
"How old are your kids?" he had asked me.
"Gabrielle just turned seven and Seth is two." I had proudly gloated.
"Oh God you have a two year old?" he had asked. "Three year olds are a pain in the ass!"

"Not my kid," I had retaliated. "Seth is cute adorable and well behaved!"
"I have never seen a three year old that wasn't a pain in the ass." He retorted.

"You'll see," I said. "They'll be here on Sunday."

The following Sunday, Mack, both children and I were seated for our Mothers Day dinner at the club following church. Mack's parents were not in attendance because they were in Florida.

There was a small window in the kitchen door where Jay could look out from his duties and see us at our table. I kept looking up at the window to see him glancing out at us. I was so obviously not into the meal that even Gabrielle noticed that I was preoccupied with the guy in the kitchen. It was not a great Mothers Day celebration. I really did not want to be in the company of my family at all and the entire family picked up on it.

A week after Mothers Day, there was another golfing event that Jay even participated in. Following the play, everyone got together in the club house and socialized. Mack and I were sitting at the bar drinking beer when Jay joined us. Everything started out fine and we were all getting along fine. As the levels of alcohol increased so did the familiarity.
Suddenly Jay decided that we should go to a neighboring town to drink at the bowling alley. So up we all got and moved our triangle to the neighboring bar.

When we arrived at the bowling alley we continued to drink. Then suddenly Mack decided to change the course of everything.
"It is not right for a mother of two children to be tending bar, don't you agree?" he had asked Jay,
Jay responded, "I don't see the problem."
"Well, I do," Mack responded. "She has two small children that she needs to be home for."
"She is home for them in the morning, until she has to come to the club." Jay had retaliated. "Jim covers the bar on the weekend; she doesn't even have to work then."
"It is not appropriate that she is tending bar!" Mack said as voice was beginning to rise.
I was sitting there wondering if these two had forgotten that I was there.
"Mack it is what I want to do right now. I like it." I had chimed in.

"Charlie, your kids miss you, and it is not appropriate for you to be gone every night." Mack had argued.

Mack was actually tap dancing around the truth; he was so proficient in doing that. He was really feeling threatened by Jay, the attention that I was getting, the independence that I was displaying and he did not want to be saddled with the kids while I worked.

Their argument continued, each of them becoming a little more indignant with their dialogue and their voices rising with each statement.

We were all three intoxicated and the bickering finally reached the point that I decided that I was not going to listen to one more word of it. I got up from the table, leaving my beer I walked out of the bar. I just started walking. The more I walked the angrier I became.

I was walking towards Fredericks that was a full ten miles away.

'What do those two morons think they are doing' I mused over in my mind. 'This is my decision not theirs and they were carrying on as if I had no say in this decision!'

Suddenly I did not want either one of them to find me and I got off the only road adjoining this town to Fredericks. This was farm country so there was no risk of danger that a stranger might abduct me but it was far from safe. I slid into the newly planted fields, and surrounding brush. It was black as pitch out there but I didn't care. I walked, and I walked and I walked! I stumbled into barb wire that I had to get around, through ditches full of over growth, through clods of turned soil, and I had to get around a creek or two. When I came to a creek I had to go back to the road to cross a bridge and then I slid back into the blackness. I got more than half way when I decided this might not have been such a brilliant idea. I came upon a really small community and looked for a pay phone to call one of my friends to come get me but there were no pay phones. At that point I sat down for a minute to rest and smoked a cigarette. Weighing my options, I realized that I had none. I got back on my feet and continued my journey on foot through the fields and ditches toward Fredericks.

I was within three miles of Fredericks and one of my best friend's apartment. I could see the lights of Fredericks and I knew that I was going to make it. Then suddenly a great wind came up, the sky was filled with lightning and the power lines above me were whining with the force of the approaching storm. Suddenly I was frightened. This was Illinois in the spring and I knew that I could get seriously injured if this storm got too severe. My compulsion was to run but I no longer had the strength. I plunged forward, one foot in front of the other, watching the lightening and listening to the howling wind. I don't think I even prayed that night I just dug down into my guts and said to myself, 'keep moving.'

At about 5:00 am I stumbled up to my girlfriend's front door. She was awake. Everyone was awake. Mack was awake, Jay was awake, the sheriff was awake, and they all showed up at Veronica's home after she phoned them all to tell them that I had been found.

My white tennis shoes were now black; the scrunch socks that I had worn the day before on the golf course were black and covered with residual vegetation, and my legs were covered with scratches from the barbed wire and thorny plants that I had trudged through.
Veronica put her arms around me. "Where the hell have you been?" she asked me.
"Mack and Jay have been looking for you all night long! The sheriff is looking for you! Mack has been here on and off all night to see if I had heard from you!"
"They pissed me off." I simply stated. "I walked back."
"You walked from the Ambassador Bowling Alley here?" she asked me incredulously.
"Yes," I said as I began to pull off my filthy socks and shoes.
Mack and Jay chided in, "You scared the living shit out of us. What were you thinking?"
"You both pissed me off!" I retorted.
"Where were you really," Mack demanded. "We have been up and down that road about fifty time and never saw you."
The very thought of Mack spending the entire night with Jay was actually quite funny to me. They really had no use for one another but the absence of me had made them strangely bond if only for a few hours.
"I was in the fields." I flatly stated. "Look at my shoes."

Everyone was satisfied that I was home and safe. The storm that I miraculous had beaten came rolling in and I went home with Mack. Unbeknownst to

the rest of them is that although it seemed an extreme and dangerous thing to do, I found strength in learning that I had found my own sense of survival and more importantly a determination that I had not known that I possessed prior to that night.
While those around me thought that I had flipped my cork I took an enormous amount of pride in the accomplishment.

Soon after the ten mile pitch black hike in the night, I conceded and quit the bartending job. It seemed like the thing to do at the time to appease Mack but I missed Jay.
I returned to talk to Jay and it was then that we started to sneak away to be together when ever we could. It was not long before the friendship became more than a friendship and we became intimate.

Mack and I had not had sex for a very long time. It infuriated Mack, but I could not overcome the years of repressed anger. I was starving for something from somewhere and Jay became the solution.
"I want a separation." I had said to Mack.
I did not ask for a divorce, I asked for a separation.

I was taking the children to my friend Susan's home when I snuck away with Jay and while I was with Jay and providing Mack with a babysitting service, he was poisoning the minds of my family.
I don't really know what he said but I know that he cried a lot and said things that were not flattering to me. He forgot in these bawl baby sessions that I had been an impeccable parent to my children and that I had given ten years of my life to his control.
I wanted a separation and that was not conducive to the Hunsdorfer image! Mack did nothing but whine.
He went to Ellie, he went Uncle Howard, he went to our friends, he called his parents, and he went anywhere he thought he might find sympathy.

His ultimate solution was that he would go to Florida; of course that's where his parents were and his business was failing in Fredericks. I was to stay in Fredericks.

During these very turbulent days when I thought that Mack was at the office, he had to have come back to the farm to listen in on my telephone calls with Jay.

He knew verbatim what Jay and I had said to one another and it was then that Mack learned that my relationship with Jay had gone beyond friendship to one that made me an adulterous.

I did not know however that he knew this for some time.

I went to the local attorney to have the 'Shared Parental Agreement' drafted. Mack was to take the children for the summer while I found employment and got on my feet. The children were to be returned in the fall for the school year and we would share visitation rights for all holidays. Having made all of these decisions, I was at peace.

While driving my car one day, I rolled down the window and turned the radio on to a deafening volume. My heart sang with glee as the radio roared out it's tunes. I was finally going to be free!

I was in total control of my own life now and I could do what I wanted, go where I wanted, say what I wanted, and spend time with whom ever I wanted. Susan and I took the children to the beach and built a huge sand castle in the sand with them. We built a mote and a channel of water that the children could drop buckets of water into to allow the water to run into the mote. It was one of the most memorable days for me with the children, and on the way home I told Seth to get back into his car seat. He was just big enough to unlock the straps and crawl free. He refused to get back into the restraint, so I pulled the car over and got out to restrain the rebellious child. He was wailing that he did not want to sit in the car seat. "If you don't stay in this car seat I will have to spank your butt!" I had said to him. The unhappy child stayed in his car seat for the remainder of the ride home. I rarely spanked my children but if I threatened to they knew that they had better comply.

It was the following week that Skye called and asked me to travel with him to Nashville.

"We have had a lot of fun together, and I may not have the chance to spend time with you again since you and Mack are splitting up." He said to me. "I'll fly up and we can take the Audi to Nashville. We can honky tonk again for a night and then drive to Florida and you can catch a flight back to Illinois."

"I can't do that. I have no money for a flight anywhere right now." I responded.

"I'll buy your ticket back." He said, "This will also make it easier for Mack so that he won't have to drive to Florida with the car and take two small kids at the same time."

It made perfect sense to me at the time, so I agreed.

Jay told me not to go, even my mother told me not to go, but I still trusted Mack to a degree and I couldn't see the harm in it.

So when Skye arrived with his friend, I left the unsigned "Shared Parental Agreement" on the kitchen counter and left for Nashville.

Chapter 18

In the end there was no custody battle. My Illinois attorney got alimony for me, Mack had possession of the children which I have learned is 9/10th of the law and it was clear to me that my Florida attorney was being paid by the Hunsdorfers to *not* represent me. But by the same token, 9/10th of law also applied to possession of property which I had.

After three months of separation from my children I could do this no longer. The attorney bills were stock piling which intimated me. I was beaten emotionally by the absence of the children and the death of the dog. I did not know what more to do but I knew that I could not stay in the fight.

My family offered no support either financially or emotionally, and I felt totally alone fighting a war against a great monster. I knew that Mack would drag me through hours of humiliation because of my emotional history and the years of counseling. He would discredit me any way he could even if he had to use the ten mile night walk. He would stop at nothing to make me look unstable and I knew that I was powerless to fight the almighty 'Hunsdorfer' image and their money.

After three months, I called Mack and told him I would give him custody but I could bear the separation no longer. On the advice of my Illinois attorney, I had phoned my children daily, but I really felt that this hurt them more than helped them because it only made them miss me all the more. After phoning Mack, he purchased a flight ticket for me to fly from Indianapolis to Tampa and he even picked me up at the airport and put me up in a Holiday Inn near my 'attorneys' office.

Mack was grieving and he hated what this was doing to me. I think he still thought that I would cave and ask for a reconciliation but that never happened.

We all congregated into my 'attorneys' office and there were Mack's four attorneys sitting at a conference table. All the introductions were made and everyone sat around a conference table to duke out the custody provisions. Somehow this process took a total of three days.

"Mack, I want to see my children!" I had said to him through my tears that would not stop.

"You can see them after you have signed the papers." He responded.
"My children are three minutes from here and I want to see them!" I said again.
"After you sign the papers." He replied, and he would not budge.
He had them tucked away at his parent's home and I had no way of knowing where they lived so I was left at his mercy to materialize them eventually.

I cried non stop for three days knowing that I was giving my children away. I spent as little time as possible inside the offices and conference room and stood on the outside balcony of the very impressive legal office, smoking, crying, blowing my nose and crying some more until it was time for the final signing of the mounds of paper work that the attorneys had generated.
I sat at the great table and looked at the paperwork through my tears. It was agreed that we would alternate holidays and share travel expenses… etc. None of that meant diddly squat to me, I was giving my children away and I wasn't sure I had the emotional strength to see this through.

At one point when we had broken for lunch, Mack took me out to a restaurant and we sat at a table across from one another and actually talked civilly to one another. It was then that he told me about my conversation with Jay that he had heard every word of.
He denied Skye having any knowledge of the abduction, which I knew was a lie and I knew that he would not have pulled the abduction off at all if not for his parents and of course Patrick who knew the legal system so that Mack and family could be coached through a legal abduction.

My 'attorney' came out for the final signing of the custody papers and said, "You are doing your children such a great service by agreeing to this."
At the final signing of the papers, I read a legal phrase that when signed stated that I was not under duress. I went ballistic. "I can't sign this!" I ranted through my hysterical tears. "What the hell do you stupid bastard attorneys constitute as duress, because I am seriously under extreme duress?"
I have no memory of their response because my grief was so intense. I only know that I signed the papers because I knew that Mack would not allow me to see them until I did. I was in close proximity to my children for three days and denied the right to see them.

That manipulation in and of itself was cruel, unfair, and in truth reckless given my mental state of mind.

Following the signing of the papers, Mack and I went with the attorneys to a nearby pub for drinks. This was *just* what I wanted to do, hang out with a bunch of legal bastards that had just robbed me of my beautiful children. But I was still at Mack's mercy so I had to tag along The attorneys were quick to tell us what a noble thing we had done for the well being of our children. That statement nearly crazed me to the point of justifiable homicide. I desperately wanted to grab one of them by the throat and squeeze the breath out him. I knew all too well what Mack had just done. Nothing was ever going to fill the cavern in the hearts of my children that Mack had just dug for them.

We finally returned to my motel room and Mack left to get the children as he had promised. When they arrived, Gabrielle was all over me with hugs. Seth did not know what to do so he behaved badly, and jumped all over the bed in an effort to show off. We finally got him settled down and I was able to spend some constructive time together with them.

When it was time for me to return to Illinois, Mack agreed to let me take the children with me for a short visit. He even paid for the air fare since I had no money. We had a lengthy layover in Atlanta and there I was with only enough money to get my car out of long term parking with two hungry small children. If not for the kindness of some well prepared travelers that shared their provisions I don't know what I would have done.

We landed in Indianapolis where my car was in long term parking and the three of us made the trip back to Fredericks where we were greeted by Jay who was awaiting my return.

It was not long enough but it was better than nothing. At the end of the visit, Jay and I packed the children up and returned them by car to Atlanta, GA where Mack met us as we had previously agreed. The next visit would not take place until Thanksgiving; three months later.

After turning the children back over to Mack, I think I cried all the way to the Georgia state line. This was the greatest heartache I had ever endured in my life, and now when I see a family that has lost a child to death, I cannot even imagine their grief.

I had learned to do artificial fingernails through Donna who had owned her own salon for some time. Although I was not licensed it was not required in Illinois at that time, so I went to a neighboring town and obtained a position as a manicurist and nail sculpture in the evenings and went to work in the factory where Jay worked during the day. I wasn't getting rich but I was getting by.

The stack of applications was very thick at the factory but the office manager was a friend of mine and Mack's and she put my application on top and put a good word in for me. Consequently I found employment there. It was physically exhausting because I lifted pallets of bags used for grain, dog food, seeds, etc., and I learned that I had muscles that had never ached so severely in my life. Eventually the hard work helped to occupy my mind as well as improve my mental health. I was feeling better because I was forced to move forward, and exercise as we all know is a stress reliever. In time I actually began to enjoy the job.
So I went to the plant at 7:00 am each morning, left the plant at 3:00 pm, went home to shower and change and got to the salon at 5:00 pm. The salon was a forty five minute drive from Fredericks and located in a mall, so I generally left the salon by 9:00 pm and then I would drive back to Fredericks where I would meet Jay and Susan at the only bar in town. We would have a few drinks, go home and do it all again the next day.

The salon was fully staffed with the strangest group of people I had ever met, but they were incredibly fun to be around. There were two gay guys that were hair dressers; one had put himself through beauty school performing as a drag queen. (He was the unacceptable son to an overbearing mother who was married to a Baptist minister.) The other was not as gay and probably somewhat bi-sexual. There was a female that was multi-sexual, I suspect she might have done farm animals if prompted, and she developed a crush on me. I eventually found her to be intimidating if not down right repulsive. And then there was a reasonably normal receptionist, another female hair dresser, and the salon manager. It was a flamboyant group of personnel and

I really enjoyed this job as well. My clients fell in love with me and my work and I soon had a pretty full schedule.

This was a strange time in my life because my grief was still very paramount but I felt some sense of satisfaction and self worth from my work. I was slowly becoming stronger and my confidence was growing each day. The most frustrating thing that I could not control was excessive under arm perspiration. I could not speak of my children or even think about them without my underarms becoming saturated. There were many nights, in the dead of winter, as I drove to the salon that I had the air conditioning vents blowing full blast in to my underarms in an effort to dry them before I arrived for work. This condition lasted a long time.

Jay was still working at the country club and he would prepare a meal for me and sneak it home so that we did not have to purchase a lot of groceries. He was still trying to move in and I was still packing him up to live out of his car. I was still legally married to Mack and even I saw this as inappropriate. Jay was not liked, approved of or accepted by my family. Danielle felt that he was beneath me and basically told him as much to his face. Uncle Howard said nothing, but it was what he didn't say that made his opinion of Jay so obvious. So I basically just went on with my survival and did not interact with my family at all. Uncle Howard arrived at the duplex to my surprise one afternoon just to see how I was doing. I was sitting at the dinette table drinking a beer when he arrived.
He made the appropriate conversation and then advised me to be careful and not let the alcohol provide an answer. Sage and well meaning advice that I did not head. If alcohol were to have been a problem I would have abused it while I was living through hell with Mack.

Then one day, Jay showed up with something even better than beer! He cut me a line of cocaine and I timidly snorted the white substance. Wow! I liked that stuff. This would have become a much better choice for addiction. Fortunately Jay and I could hardly afford to pay attention, so it never became a problem but it certainly could have.

Eventually the three months passed and it was time for the children to return for Thanksgiving with me. Jay and I packed up and drove to Atlanta where we picked up the elated children. It was so obvious to me how desperately these children missed the presence of their mother in their daily lives that it simply broke my heart. But there was nothing more that I felt I could do for them. So we spent the four days together and I prepared a turkey and dressing holiday feast. It was a very nice visit, virtually uneventful except that I took both children to the salon and had their hair cut to show them off and then it was time to return them to their father. Once again Jay and I drove back to Atlanta where we met Mack and then they were gone. The grief that I had managed to control was suddenly back and once again I could not stop the uncontrollable tears.

Soon after the holiday meal, Mack called to reprimand me because my Thanksgiving dinner was not presented to the children at noon. Through my entire childhood, Aunt Elise had prepared holiday feast that were not consumed until mid day. I had adopted the same practice and continue to do so to this day.
"What the hell is it to you what time my Thanksgiving dinner was presented?" I had asked him sarcastically.
"Well the kids need to eat earlier than that." He had retorted.
"Oh go to hell Mack!" I responded, "They didn't starve to death and you no longer have the right to tell me what to do, and certainly not to tell me when I should have a damn meal prepared in my house."
I hung the phone up.

Sometime between Thanksgiving and Christmas, Mack returned for a final divorce hearing that would free him from the measly alimony that he was paying me and we divided marital property at that time. I agreed to return the office equipment that meant nothing to me, and he agreed to give me the equity in the duplex when it was sold. The remaining marital assets were divided such as kitchen pans and furnishings and the divorce was now emanate.

Soon Christmas was upon us and it was not a pleasant time for me. All of the Christmas ornaments had been left at the big house. I phoned my attorney and asked him if I could get back in to get the holiday things that I had foolishly not gotten.

Mr. Ebers was very irritated with me and said." I told you to get everything that you wanted months ago!"

"I know but I wasn't thinking about Christmas last June," I reasoned.

"Well you can't get back in there now." He said. "You have already made your final decisions in property settlements. Anything that you left in that house is history now."

So Jay and I had a very un-ornate Christmas that year. It was probably best since the children were not there any way and it really did not feel much like a joyful time. Jay and I had a small gift exchange between us and went to his parent's home for Christmas dinner. We did however go to the salon's Christmas party which was too much fun watching Jay attempting to cope with the gay guys and the very bazaar multi-sexual girl.

The final divorce papers were not signed by the Judge until after the first of the year due to Mr. Ebers wisdom. He wanted to insure that any tax return that Mack filed would automatically become half mine therefore he held the final judgment papers until after January 1st, 1988. Although Mr. Ebers was disappointed that the custody battles did not bring the national notoriety that he had hoped for, he did a very good job as legal council for me. This may have been in part because he was practicing law under the senior attorney's law firm that was also the attorney whose son's life had been saved by my Aunt Elise years before. But to his credit I think he was the type of attorney that was conscientious, did his absolute best for the benefit of his client and did not like to loose. He honestly did not like me personally and he had told Mack's Illinois attorney early on that he did not think that I really wanted my children I just wanted what I could get from the almighty Hunsdorfers. Even my own attorney did not see through the facade that I had put on to make them all believe that I was strong and stable. I was terrified in those early days that any sign of weakness that I displayed would be used to make me look unstable and unfit. So even in the eyes of my attorney I had done too good a job performing for the outside world.

The divorce was finalized after the first of the year and the duplex was put up for sale. The tenants on the other side wanted to purchase it so it was only a matter of time before it was sold. The attorneys were now sending me their final billing which I could not possibly pay until the property was sold. Mr. Ebers knew this and did not harass me about it but Joe Johnson the attorney that did *nothing* to represent me became belligerent and harassed me on the phone.

"You can't get blood from a turnip!" I had argued to him.

"Well I don't want blood from a turnip!" he exclaimed, "I want cash from you!"

"I don't have any cash, nor will I have until the property sells so you might as well cool your jets!" I had angrily retorted.

He threatened me with some legal mumbo jumbo and I hung up on him.

The next visit with the children did not occur until the following Easter. Once again Jay and I loaded up to pick up the children in Atlanta but this time we had to work through some serious glitches. Jay could get time away from the factory without any problems but they were not willing to let me have the time off to get my children.

I sat in the break room crying not knowing what in the hell to do now. How was I going to get my children? Mack would never just hand them over to Jay. I had to be there.

I went to the plant manager and I begged him to give me the day off. "I have to go to Atlanta to get my children." I had pleaded to him. "Please I have to go!"

"I can't do without you." He responded. "If it was Julie or one of the other girls that are not as skilled as you then I could let them go, but you are too valuable and I need you here."

This totally confused me. What made me so proficient at a factory job? 'An ape could do what I do,' I thought to myself. But he was not going to budge.

Word spread quickly through out the plant that I was not able to pick my children up because Joe would not give me the time off.

My previous experience in Fredericks had been rubbing shoulders with those that were better than the general populous of this small town, but I quickly learned that the working stiffs were not of the same make up. To my disbelief, relief and grave gratitude, two of my co-workers came to me and offered to work my shift so that I might be able to go get my children. I could not believe this! We went to Joe the manager and asked if this could be done. He agreed that if the two girls were willing to work my shift and were willing to give up their day off then I could go. I was so unbelievably indebted to the women that were willing to do this for me, I could not believe it. This was Fredericks where no one had ever gone to any length to make me even feel welcome, but now these people were actually willing to make sacrifices for me. Clearly I had not socialized with the right class of people.

Jay and I loaded his fathers Suburban that we were borrowing for this trip as we prepared to make the journey south one more time. This time however I had something to do before we left. I contacted the local florist and told them to deliver to the factory two small floral arrangements, each with a thank you card and I wanted them delivered to the factory while the girls worked my shift. I later learned that the girls were as surprised by my show of gratitude as I had been by there willingness to help me. Some short lived friendships were born as a result of this.

Jay and I retrieved the children and returned to Fredericks. We celebrated Easter with an Easter egg hunt and dinner but I did not go crazy with the Easter thing. I have never found a correlation between a bunny rabbit, colored eggs and the resurrection of Christ! One simply does not compliment the other. At least at Christmas, Santa brings gifts as the Kingsmen had brought to the birth of Jesus.

Over the Easter visit Gabrielle had her eighth birthday and we had a party to celebrate her birth and then all too soon it was time to return to Atlanta to once again return them. This time however, Jay and I attempted to entertain the children a bit rather than making them endure the twelve hour drive, just to climb into another vehicle and travel another twelve hours. So as we traveled south we made stops at tourist attractions.
We took them to see Ruby Falls, Lookout Mountain, and Santa's Rock Gardens, but nothing I said or did would bring Gabrielle out of her somber withdrawn mood. She was not happy and nothing that I did was going to improve her disposition. She was old enough to know that she was going back to Florida and sight seeing did nothing to dissuade her attitude of grief and anger. This display of emotional dissatisfaction was further exacerbated by the fact that she had absolutely no use for Jay!

As we approached Atlanta, GA, Jay looked into his rear view mirror and commented to me. "Your daughter is crying, you might want to say something to her."

I didn't have a clue what I was supposed to say to her, but I crawled from the front of the Suburban to the back and cradled her in my arms. Seth had wet his pants because he was so distressed by the return trip and all I could do was hold them in my arms and cradle them. I sat in the back and held my children until we arrived at our designated spot to meet Mack.

"I am so sorry," was all I could say to them through my own tears, "I have to bring you back."

Mack arrived with a woman this time. He had a new girlfriend and the two of them took my children and returned to Florida. Once again I cried through the entire state of Georgia, but as I traveled back to Fredericks this time I made a long over due decision. I had to get closer to my children.

Part 3

C. R. Perk

Chapter 19

With my return to Fredericks I said to Jay, "I have got to get closer to my children and I am moving south. I don't want to move to Florida though. I hate that state and everything it represents to me. Maybe I can find a place somewhere in southern Georgia."
"Am I going with you?" he asked.
"I thought you would." I responded.
"I'm not going anywhere with out more of a commitment." He said to me.
"Just what kind of a commitment are you looking for?" I asked.
"I think we should get married." He stated very simply.
This sent mega rays of fear through me. I was only barely divorced from Mack and I wasn't so sure I was ready for this bold of a move, but I was even more terrified of going south alone. I had thought that Jay would just come along.
"I really think that is a bit premature don't you?" I responded.
"Well I am not just going to pick up and leave my jobs, friends and family to run off with you somewhere with out some type of commitment. If you won't marry me then I am not going."
So as a solution to get closer to my kids and not have to do it alone, I agreed to marry him.
And then I changed my mind, and the day after that I changed my mind again, and the day after that I changed my mind again… and so on.

We set the date for May 7th and bought our rings. I selected my gown which was black, white and red, Jay rented a black tuxedo with a red cumber bun and handkerchief for his lapel. His mother was appalled by the color selections, but I was not wearing a white or even a cream gown for my second wedding. The black probably was a reflection of my subconscious feelings that predicted the inevitable doom of the marriage.

The participation of the factory workers in preparation for this event was staggering. Our co-workers knew that at the close of the ceremony that we would no longer be employed there and that we were going to leave Fredericks forever but that had no impact on their assistance.

The wedding was a church wedding, followed by a brief stop at a tavern so that we might make a late entrance to the reception which was located on a farm. The farm was lovely with a pond and Weeping Willow trees, there was a barn for the band and food to be displayed, a small cake was provided from somewhere and a money tree was erected for donations instead of gifts. It was really quite an affair.
The farm was an offering from one of the co-workers, the band was volunteered and the food was prepared by well wishers. Mine and Jay's only expenses were the pork fillets that were prepared by a family friend and the six kegs of beer that were brought in for the celebration.

Another co-worker who was a gifted vocalist sang at the church for the ceremony. It was a small and closed ceremony with only family, our best man and maid of honor.
Susan was my maid of honor. As I dressed in the church and prepared to be married again, I said to Susan, "I don't think that I am doing the right thing."
"Then don't do it!" she exclaimed.
"Susan, I have to. I have gone this far and I am not going to leave Jay at the alter." I responded.
So moments later I was making my way down the isle and met Jay before the minister.
Ellie was the only member of my family to attend the small ceremony and she went with us to the tavern following the vows but she did not attend at the reception.

The party was splendid. I kicked my shoes off at some point and soiled the bottom of my dress to the point of ruin. Jay removed his dress shoes and replaced them with a pair of Budweiser slip-on tennis shoes. The band was nothing spectacular, but acceptable for free and every one got drunk, some got stoned and everyone had a fabulous time.
The following morning feeling a bit rough, Jay and I went back to the farm to clean the disaster sight up and learned that two taps had been stolen from the kegs.

This slowed our progress down a bit and we had to do some research to learn who had stolen them, but eventually we did and at the risk of Jay kicking someone's ass they were eventually returned.

After the ceremony, Jay and I began putting furniture in storage, and packing our personal belongings for our journey south.
I had taken a fifteen hundred dollar loan against my car for traveling expenses and left the title with the bank in Fredericks. I knew that the property closing would be soon and I would be able to buy my title back.

So after packing up to leave, finding a home for our cat Bud,(short for Budweiser) and saying our final good-byes to friends and family, we left Fredericks behind and headed south on Interstate 57.
We had no idea where we were going to stop and set up house but that was alright, we were young and it was an adventure. I asked that we not take the Interstate south at 24 in Chattanooga to Interstate 75 because it was a direct shot to Atlanta and Florida. We moved south through Alabama and southern Georgia in hopes of finding a location that was promising for employment. We saw nothing very promising especially in Alabama. Southern Georgia wasn't much better and eventually we crossed the Florida state line at the Panhandle.

I cried as we crossed the state border. I did not want to live in Florida. Forget that there were a thousand other cities in Florida that we could live other than Mack's nest hole with his entire family, all of which had migrated to mama's door, I did not want to move here.
But we continued south in the state of Florida and stopped in Alachua to rest for the night. We both exited the car and went into the motel to check out a room. After reserving a room we went back to the car to move it closer to our room and retrieve our luggage and it was then that Jay realized that he had locked the keys in the car. After going back into the lobby of the motel to ask for a coat hanger we attempted to pick the lock on the door. Nothing worked, and we were unable to gain entry again. We had no road side service such as AAA and it never entered either of our minds to telephone a lock smith. I continued repeatedly to pick the lock and that was when I first witnessed the monster that lived within Jay.

He lost his temper and began to rant at me, cussing and threatening to bust out the window.

"This is my car and you are not busting out the window." I had shouted at him.

"Well what the f-ck do you suggest we do?" he had screamed at me.

"I don't know, but you are not busting out the window!" I yelled back.

His tantrum continued and he repeatedly threatened to bust out the window. He was like an enraged bull and I could not get him to calm down and use his head instead his fist.

I continued to attempt to unlock the car with the coat hanger and after about three hours a policeman finally came cruising by. He drove by slowly as he watched me attempt to perform a break and entry. He rolled his window down as he approached me standing by the car.

"It's about time you got here," I said, "if I'd been a car thief I would have been gone hours ago," I attempted to teased the policeman.

"What's up? The policeman asked me.

"Our keys are locked in the car." I confessed. "Got any ideas?"

The very nice police produced a very illegal slim jim and within a few minutes we were back into the car with out having broken the window.

I thanked the policeman profoundly, and he left us.

The situation had not been one of life or death. We could have simply gone to our room and addressed the problem in the morning. It wasn't as if we had someplace that we had to be or an appointment that we had to keep. We were on a trip to an unknown destination and I was astonished by Jay's over reactive rage and immaturity.

We continued our journey south and finally Jay said, "We are going to Ft. Myers where my grandparents have a trailer. We can stay in the trailer and figure out what to do next."

I suspect that Jay had humored me all the way to Florida knowing that we would find no appropriate place to stop and also knowing that he had this refuge when we finally had to make a decision. So we drove the remainder of the interstate until we arrived in Ft. Myers, some ninety miles south of my children. As we approached the main stretch of highway where much of the industry was located in Ft. Myers and I saw all the lights I became terrified. I could not possibly drive through this thriving metropolis, I was a county girl! There were no traffic lights in Fredericks and not many in my home town; this was going to be way too fast paced for me.

We arrived at the trailer and Jay found the hidden key and unlocked the trailer. It was no paradise but it was a place to start. So we moved in with our minimal provisions.
The trailer was fully equipped with cooking utensils, beds, a bathroom, telephone and a washer and dryer. I began setting up house, did our laundry and purchased minimal grocery provisions.

Immediately following our arrival to Ft. Myers, Jay had to show me the beach so we headed for Ft. Myers Beach with our cheap beer to watch the sun set.
I sat beside the gulf in the sand and watched as the sun began its descent. My left hand was positioned beside me in the sand and I looked down at it. There on the fourth finger of my left hand was the sparkling new band that Jay had just placed on my finger only days before. The gold that glittered in the fading sun light looked lovely, but the light in my heart was not so bright. 'What have I done?' I asked myself.

We were going to run out of money soon so we began to look for jobs, and in shear desperation I contacted Danielle that I knew was very hung up on obtaining jewelry that had belonged to Aunt Elise and I offered her the opportunity to purchase a very pricy watch that had been given to me by Uncle Howard years earlier shortly after the death of Aunt Elise.

The watch was high end and very heavy white gold with twenty four diamonds surrounding the face of the watch. The total carats were in access of a full carat. At the time it was appraised at about $9000.00, today it is probably worth three times that amount. I asked Danielle if she was interested in purchasing the watch for a minimal amount on a monthly basis. She was very interested, so I shipped the watch to her. She in turn sent me the $250.00 as agreed. She sent one payment. I would have been better off taking it to a pawn shop.

I quickly contacted my children and told them that I had moved to Florida and wanted to know when I could pick them up. A visitation schedule was agreed to between Mack and I and the children were soon in my care again.

The trailer park was small and located right beside a motel and Jay knew all the tricks to survival when you actually have nothing, and to my horror he snuck into the pool at the motel with the kids so that they could swim. I just knew that they would get caught but they never did.

Jay was very good to my children, and in many ways he spoiled them rotten. While Jay bonded with Seth, Gabrielle still had grave reservations about him. I think she thought he was the reason that her mommy and daddy were not married anymore and she would not forgive him that, but she would swim with him.

The children were picked up on Fridays and returned on Sunday nights to Mack and at that time Mack was still meeting me halfway with visitation even though the distance was now reduced from fifteen hundred miles to ninety miles.

Jay found employment at a restaurant right down the street and he started to cook nights. I apprehensively over came my fear to drive in this booming big little town and soon found a job at a local marina as a service writer. I worked during the day.

So as we gradually managed to get on our feet we decided to leave the trailer and moved into an area in Ft. Myers that is referred to as "Crime Manor". I could not get over the price of rental properties in Florida so we took the cheapest rental we could find and this was located in the higher end of Crime Manor, but you did not leave your doors unlocked.

For some unknown reason, Jay decided to sell my car and he made arrangements to sell it to one of his co-workers at the restaurant. He actually gave the car to the guy without payment. I was crazed! "What are you doing, we need that car and you have no way to get our money!" I had yelled at him.

"Oh Horace won't screw us." He had reassured me.

Well not surprisingly, Horace vanished with my car and when Jay finally caught up with him the car had been taken to Miami where the head gasket blew and the car was abandoned. I was livid and I wanted my money. You find that worthless son of bitch and get my money I had told Jay.

When Jay could no longer find Horace at his work place, he suddenly materialized in the county stockade.

We lived in the dump for about six months before the duplex finally sold and suddenly we felt rich. I paid the loan off with the bank back in Fredericks and I paid my Illinois attorney fees. We also miraculously managed to finance a used car, and we moved to a much more pleasant apartment complex.

To this day I have never paid my Florida attorney. When I moved from Fredericks he lost track of me. I could see absolutely no reason why the man should be paid twice, and he charged as much for three days of work as my Illinois attorney had charged me for nine months of work. I'm sure the man was livid.

While I worked at the marina during the day, Jay was having a field day spending my money. I came home one day to a new water bed, another day to new furniture, another day to a set of graphite golf clubs that he had traded his Pings for and ultimately he bought a car, and all of this was done without my knowledge or consent.
He was doing a bang up job of going through my money while I was at work and the greatest sin is that I allowed him to do it.
Jay left his job at the restaurant and went to work for a golf course as a grounds keeper.
He made no more money but he worked day time hours now and actually liked the job.
As a result we had free golf privileges.
I was not having a very good time with my job at the marina. I was the low dog on the totem pole and I was working under two of the rudest people I had ever encountered in my life. They were down right belligerent to their customers and they intimidated the hell out of everyone. I once took a pay check to the bank and the clerk asked how I liked the job because she had heard it was a horrible place to work. She had heard absolutely right!

There was a bait shop on sight and the owner of the bait shop also offered beer. So at the close of a business day, the mechanics and yard laborers went to the bait shop for a happy hour beer. I enjoyed having a beer and getting

to know my co-workers better so I frequently went to the bait shop after work.
This seemed to annoy Jay so I even invited him to join me. That was even a worse idea because the gold eyes became suspicious again and he began to size up my co-workers.
It was not long before he started the accusations.
"Those guys want in your pants." He had ranted.
"Who wants in my pants?" I had defended myself. Not one of the techs or yard laborers had made the first advance toward me. They were nice guys that I worked with each day.

One of the managers had asked me to meet him at a park where he would be with his children over a weekend and I accepted but I also took Jay with me. One of the other workers invited us over to their home to swim, but absolutely no one had made an advance toward me. It is true that I was bonding with the personnel that I worked with and very much enjoyed their company, but no one was behaving inappropriately.
Jay did not get over his suspicions and his accusations continued.

I left the job at the marina after about six months though. Not because of Jays harassing suspicions, but because the stress level was so great that it was affecting my health. I had developed muscle spasm in my back from the two idiotic superiors and the spasms were so severe that I left in tears one day and had to go to a walk in clinic for muscle relaxers.

My next job choice was to try selling medicare supplements to senior citizens. I obtained my license and began making calls on clients. I had some wonderful visits with lonely elderly people, but I learned that I could not do the close. The close requires that you put the people into a state of fear if they are not adequately protected and then you push them for a check. I couldn't do it. No matter how poor we were, I could not do it.
I wanted to help the senior citizens, not take advantage of their fear. In four months I sold two small policies.

One day in my attempt to sale insurance, I was traveling by the marina and stopped to say hello to everyone.

I went to the service department to say hello to the two tyrants and found that they were not there. I was rather confused by this and asked one of the yard guys what had happened to them.
"You haven't heard? They were asked to leave." He said with glee in his voice.
I was shocked. I thought those two would be there forever.
"No shit?" I responded. "What happened?"
"Don't really know, they just got called to the office and the next thing anyone knew they had packed up and left." He said to me.

I left the marina that day and a plan was formulating in my head. The general manager had liked me and I had gotten along well with my co-workers. To add a feather to my cap when the customers got used to me, they like me. Truly many of the customers were so badly abused and financially raped by the duo that they had come to deal with only me, and I was still trying to figure out what a barnacle was, which was a stern drive or an inboard, and which was port from starboard. I had actually liked the work, liked my co-workers and was obsessed with winning customer approval.

I went home and got my rather miniscule resume together and drove back to the marina. I caught the general manager in the parking lot and handed him my resume.
"I really liked working here," I said to him, "but I could not work with those tyrants. I would really appreciate it if you would consider rehiring me."
The very next day I received a telephone call from the office manager offering me my old position back.
I was thrilled. No more trying to sell people insurance that they really did not need, or could not afford.

When I arrived back at the marina, I was given an increase in pay of a dollar and a half and turned loose to do what I do best, provide the best service to my customers that I possibly could. I was home again. I had found another family and it was the personnel and the customers of this work place that made me feel welcome and good about what I did each day. I was there for only six weeks when I was put in charge of the department and my official title which I selected was 'Service Coordinator'. I could not tear down an outboard motor and put it back together which would have been something that a service manager would have been expected to do, but I could coordinate and manage and I did it well. These were by far and away the happiest days of my life.

Jay was not so thrilled because he was right back to feeling threatened by all the men that I worked with, but I was happy. For once in my life I felt happy.
Then the abuse began. A little at a time but the aggression was rearing its ugly head

Chapter 20

It started with small little things like him becoming annoyed with my love of my work.
He would begin to shout at me by saying things like, "You cheated on your first husband, what is to keep from cheating on me. You know those guys at the marina want in your pants and you like it don't you?"
"No one at the marina has made the first advance toward me." I retaliated.
"Yea but they want to and you like it don't you?" he retorted.
"Jay get over it, there is nothing going on!" I yelled back at him.
He would talk himself into such a frenzy that there was nothing I could say to reassure him.
At one point he pinned me by the throat to the kitchen wall and later threw a kitchen knife at me. I took all of this in stride but found myself dreading weekends and living for the work week. I loved being at work and I hated being at home. Somehow without me ever saying a word to any of my co-workers, they knew that he was being abusive. However it would take some time before I realized it.

Then the ultimate tragedy struck. I was certain that I was unable to become pregnant. I had not used birth control since arriving in Ft. Myers over a year before.
In fact I had not seen a doctor except for the walk in clinic for the muscle spasms.
I opened the local newspaper and read about the homeless children in the area that needed homes and that opened all my maternal feelings again. I briefly entertained the thought of providing foster care to children that were homeless as a result of the feelings that this article provoked in me. I had lost my children but I might be able to provide some sense of stability to other children. My children still came to visit every other weekend, but it was not the same as having them around all the time and everyday.

I did absolutely nothing for the homeless children except to empathize with them and wish that I could cradle them in a mothers loving embrace, and the next thing I knew I was pregnant.

Reading that full page spread must have opened me up to fertility where I had somehow managed to suppress those body functions due to fear and heartache as a result of losing my own biological children. I was devastated.

I knew that I was pregnant, I felt like I was pregnant, but I refused to accept that I was pregnant. I was just beyond my third month when on the advice of a friend, and a referral, I finally contacted an obstetrician.
The doctor did not know quite what to do with me. I was a new patient so I went to consult with him in his office rather than an examination room.
"So," he said cheerfully, "we're going to have a baby."
Immediately I began to cry and shook my head in denial.
"We're not going to have a baby?" he asked me some what puzzled.
"I don't believe that I am pregnant and I don't want to be pregnant!" I declared.
"Well honey you are definitely pregnant." He flatly stated, "But you don't have to go through with the pregnancy you know."
I sat and shook my head from side to side, crying hysterically. "I can't do that."
I had already been down that road in the past. I was thirty one years old and I knew where babies come from. I could not snuff out a life because it was not convenient.
"My husband knows that I am pregnant and I can't just destroy his child. He's a country boy with simple ideas." I said through my tears.
The young pro abortion physician tried and tried to get me to reconsider but I would not budge. I would not kill another unborn child.
"Well," he finally said, "dry up those tears. We might as well be happy because we're going to have a baby."
I looked at him through my tears and asked him, "Can you do something to make me believe it's real, because I don't want to believe it, and if I don't believe that it is real I won't properly care for it."
He immediately sent me to the ultrasound room where I had a vaginal screening done.
There on the screen was the tiniest form of a human, and it was growing in my womb.
There was no more denial. I had a growing embryo in my womb.

Through the Eyes of Betsy McCall

I went to the marina and informed my co-workers that I was pregnant. It was a shock to them all but accepted and everything went forward as usual. The lift operator brought a customer to the office to do a repair order and I prepared to take down all the pertinent information.
"Your name, address, phone, and what type of boat do you have?" I asked him.
"I have a 10 meter Trojan." The customer replied.
"If you'd used one of those you wouldn't be in this fix." The lift operator said which created a disruption of hysterical laughter amongst everyone in the service department.
I just laughed with everyone else despite the rise of blood to my face. I had learned that the lift operator whose name was Roger was always quick with wit and sarcasm. He was one of the more fun people that I worked with.

My doctor got me started on my prenatal vitamins, I quit drinking all together but I never even attempted to stop smoking. I had turned out alright, I rationalized to myself and all of my other siblings were alright and no one even thought about cigarettes being a deterrent when we were conceived. So I continued to smoke a pack and a half a day throughout the entire pregnancy. The mental rationalization was not really as effective as I wanted everyone to believe. I secretly in my heart feared for the fetus and the effect the cigarettes might have on its development. I had not smoked excessively with Gabrielle and Seth so I did not fret so through their gestations, but I was not so excited about the child that now grew within me.
I did not know what I would do with the child when it inevitably arrived. I had no knowledge of the area child care facilities, and I knew nothing of the areas pediatricians.
I once was lying in a bath as I caressed my swollen abdomen and I spoke to the child that I now knew was a female. Emily would be her name, and I spoke to her as I rubbed the skin above her. "What ever in the world am I going to do with you?" I had asked her.
She offered no response except to reposition herself as an elbow or a knee rolled across the top of my uterus.
I was terrified of the prospect of loving another child, I did not have room in my life for an infant, and I would have been totally content with out this intrusion. I was bringing a child into a marriage that I knew was doomed

to failure, and I just could not figure out what the prospects possibly would become.

When I shared the knowledge that I was pregnant with Gabrielle and Seth, Gabrielle immediately began to cry. Seth really did not understand that another child was coming into his space but Gabrielle did and it frightened her because she thought the new baby would replace her.
"You won't love us anymore." She had said to me.
"Oh yes I will sweet heart and you know what else, so will the baby. When I come to get you she will jump up and down in the car because she will be so excited to see you." I had said to her.
"Really?" She asked me
"Really," I responded, "you'll see."
So Gabrielle and Seth accepted the inevitable birth of their half sibling. I tried for their sake to make it seem as if it was to be the happiest event to occur in their young lives.

Mack was sterilized after the birth of Seth, and had now remarried. When his new wife learned that I was pregnant she immediately had to have another child. Mack had our two children and she already had a son that was Seth's age, but when I became pregnant then she too needed to become pregnant. To my astonishment, Mack had his vasectomy reversed and soon after the birth of Emily there was another pregnancy in the works. I felt sorrow for Gabrielle and Seth having to deal with so many changes but there was nothing to be done but to deal with the circumstances as they developed.

Although my pregnancy with Emily presented some emotional and personal conflicts, I was not so miserable with my life as a whole through her gestation. I worked through out the pregnancy and found a following from my customers as her birth drew near. I was more satisfied with my life and consequently I did not blow up like the Hindenburg with her. Some said that I was radiant, but I have never felt radiant with any of my pregnancies.

The abuse from Jay stopped as my stomach swelled, and nine months later Emily was born a healthy 7lbs 10 oz. The smoking had nearly destroyed my placenta and she came a little early, but otherwise it was a normal pregnancy and delivery.

Emily was born on a Friday evening and on Saturday she appeared to be a healthy pink baby girl. Jay and I went to the nursery and requested to bring our infant to our room. We wheeled her mobil bassinette to my hospital room and I reached down and cradled my perfect new infant in my arms. I had already counted all her fingers and toes and felt fairly confident that she was a healthy perfectly developed child. As I un-wrapped her blanket I saw a lab tag on her arm that read 'baby boy Tate.' I was distraught and I rang for a nurse. The nurse arrived and I said to her, "I don't need to un-wrap this baby to tell if this is a boy child. This is my daughter and this tag says that she is a boy."

The nurse quickly scrambled to verify that Emily had been incorrectly tagged by the lab personnel. As upset as I was by this error, for the time being I overlooked the incompetence and accepted it when the corrections were made.

The following day when Jay arrived and picked up his daughter he looked at me said, "Charlie she is yellow."

He was right, she was unbelievably yellow. Emily had been born jaundice. This is a common occurrence in new born infants, but thanks to the incompetence of the hospital staff my child had been surviving with out liver function, or treatment for this condition in access of forty eight hours. Jay and I brought this to the attention of the nursing staff and they immediately carted her away. Emily's bilirubin count was dangerously high by now and I was certain that baby boy Tate had by now been treated for jaundice.

Jay had picked up Gabrielle and Seth and brought them to the hospital to see me and Emily. They couldn't hold their new sister because her jaundice was so severe that she could only be removed from the therapeutic lights long enough for me to nurse her and then immediately be returned to the lights that somehow help to disseminate the bilirubin which is a bi product of the old or un-used excessive red blood cells that the liver has failed to breakdown .properly.

I was not immediately overly concerned because Gabrielle had been born jaundice too but she had not been nearly so ill. I was allowed to take Gabrielle home with me when I was released from the hospital, and instructed to put her in a sunny window when she slept.

This time the jaundice was not so easily treated and when the insurance company would no longer pay for me to stay in the hospital, I was released.

Whether I wanted to leave or not, I had to go, but Emily could not go home with me. I was being told that I had to leave and my new born infant could not leave. They were forcing me to leave my baby!

Suddenly Emily was no longer an inconvenience, she was no longer unwanted baggage, Emily was my child whom I had bonded with through the gestation whether I had realized it or not and now the hospital and /or the insurance company was forcing us to be separated.

I walked clinging to Jay for support with my two other children trailing down the hospital corridor as I literally wailed, "Please don't make me leave my baby. Please don't make me leave my baby. Oh god Jay, don't let this happen. Please tell them that I can't leave my baby!"

Jay comforted me knowing full well that Emily had to stay for treatment and I had to leave. "It will be ok." he had tried to reassure me. "It's only until she is well enough to come home too. You can come see her when ever you want to."

There was no consoling me. No one understood the magnitude of how difficult this was for me. I had just lost custody of two children and now the powers to be expected me to leave my precious new born and just go home. Somehow my feet moved forward when my heart was left in the hospital nursery.

I had not even been released to drive, but I was still expected to somehow materialize to nurse my child, and that is exactly what I did. Every four hours I was back at the hospital to nurse her and I cried the entire time that I sat in the rocking chair cradling her and providing her with mother's milk. I drove myself to and from the hospital and on the Monday following the berthing on Friday I was right back at the marina. Jay had returned to work and I could not sit around the apartment alone. So I drove myself back to the marina.

My return to the marina was really special actually. On the company signage off of the street they had posted a birth announcement that read:

It's a girl
Emily Marie
7 lbs. 10 oz.

A salesman asked me what the hell I was doing there two days after giving berth, a technician that had been hired while I was pregnant was surprised to learn that I really did have a figure, and the girls in my office were eager to provide hugs and words of encouragement. It helped to take my mind off of the fact that I was grieving due to my separation from my new born originally unwanted child.

It was a full week before I was allowed to take my daughter home but eventually Jay and I strapped her into her infant car seat and Emily was finally instated into her own crib in our apartment. It had been a long difficult week.

Finally at home, I was quick to put my bikini back on and take Emily to the pool in her infant seat. I was only taking three weeks of maternity leave from work so I was prepared to go back looking fit and tan.
I had found a childcare facility that would actually take infants at three weeks of age so that was my goal, and I was determined to return to work as soon as possible. So at the end of the three weeks, I left her at a childcare facility, and to my astonishment I was once again reduced to tears after I had left her. I got the tears under control as I drove to work and as soon as I arrived the girls ask if I was ok with leaving her at childcare.
Immediately my eyes filled with tears again.
The girls gave me hugs and comforted me once again.

Soon I was back in full swing at the office and my clients were coming around to ask about the new baby and eventually I became more comfortable with leaving Emily in the surrogate care of others.

I took Emily to a wonderful pediatrician for follow up care following her birth and he informed me that I had to have her hearing tested.

"Why do I have to take her for a hearing test?" I asked him.
"Because her bilirubin count was so excessively high that she runs the risk of being deaf." He responded.
I was dumbfounded by this. She appeared to be perfectly normal to me and now I was being told that my daughter may be deaf.
"She may be fine," he said, "but we need to be sure."
So off I went to a clinic to have my infant daughters hearing tested. I don't understand the dynamics involved and upon observation of the testing I could not imagine how they determined that she was able to hear, but the results of the test indicated that thankfully she was not deaf.

Soon after that scare, Jay and I noticed that she did not blink. We even rapidly and aggressively ran our fingers close to her eyes to prompt a blink from her and she did not blink. We watched her eyes to see if she were attempting to follow sounds and voices but she only stared into blank space. This terrified me more than the hearing test, so I promptly took her back to her pediatrician who performed the same tests that Jay and I had already attempted and he informed me that he could not be certain that she was able to see. We would have to wait and see.

Then within Emily's first three months of life she developed severe asthma. She had been exposed to the common cold at the day care and it manifested itself into life threatening asthma. She was admitted to the hospital where she was treated with an oxygen tent, bronco dilators and steroids. It seemed however that we would only manage to get her out of the hospital and she was readmitted within another couple of months. Emily was in the hospital three times in her first year of life and the medical bills were stockpiling on Jay and me.
On one of her last visit to the hospital in this first year, I was sleeping in a chair at night and keeping vigil by her crib that looked like a cage for an animal. The steroids made her thrash and attempt to climb up the rails of her cage and it was none stop. They manifested stimulus and she could not stop the thrashing and rocking and banging and climbing and clutching. I sat in the chair helpless to help her. Her nurse entered the room and did not ask how her patient was doing, but instead asked how her mom was holding up. That was the wrong thing to do! I could not respond because I was not doing

well at all and this was all that it took was for someone to acknowledge my pain and it came boiling over.

"I can't stand seeing her like this!" I blurted out as the tears began to roll down my cheeks.

"It's hard I know because the steroids cause them to act like that." The nurse volunteered.

"But they also help to reduce the bronchial swelling, a necessary evil."

So I sat in the chair in my misery, watching my infant in hers.

After the first year we had learned a great deal about the disease and how to treat her on our own if it did not become too severe.

We began by borrowing a nebulizer from one of my co-workers whose daughter was also asthmatic, but eventually had to purchase one of our own. The nebulizer enabled us to treat the disease from home when it was not too severe but it frustrated me because it did not seem to bring enough relief to her and I felt inadequate in my effort to help her breath.

Jay and I were both smokers but immediately took our habit outdoors. Emily needed her own air space and we saw to it that she got it. Still we struggled with the asthma almost daily for a very long time. Thankfully we learned in time that she was not blind and it was an enormous relief when she visually began to respond to images and sounds.

We were upside down in medical bills, with a sick child, and the tension was taking its toll on Jays and my relationship. He was drinking too much and I was upset with his refusal to leave the golf course job to make a better living.

Eventually he was contacted by an old friend from up north who had also relocated to Florida, and that friend advised him that he could get a better paying job cutting pipe for a sprinkler company. Jay did not want to take the dirty job and lose his golf privileges but I insisted and he did make the change.

Somehow after her first birthday we managed to keep her well enough so that she did not go back to the hospital and I began trying to dig us out of the financial pit that her illness had placed us in.

I lived in fear every day that a child would come to day care with a cold and we would be right back to treating the asthma again. It was a justifiable fear because it happened repeatedly and each time that it occurred I attempted to keep it under control before going back to see her physician.

Despite the many problems that we were already attempting to overcome, Jay's insecurities began to rear their ugly heads once again. I was still dedicated to my job at the marina and as a release from the tensions at home I began to hang out with the gang at work after hours and drink a couple beers before picking up Emily and going home.
This enraged Jay and he was convinced that something was going on.
No matter how many times I attempted to reassure him, he did not believe me.
Then one night I told Jay that I was going out with the gang for drinks at there local hangout and have some drinks. After work we all went down to the pub and sat at a large table. We partied and drank and after about three hours I said to Roger the lift operator,"I think I'm in trouble, I don't think I can drive home."
With that having been said, Roger grabbed a rigger and said, "We gotta take her home, I'll drive her car and you follow to pick me up."
No arguing, no messing around, we were quickly in route to mine and Jays apartment.
When we arrived Roger walked me up to the building and as we approached the steps to the second floor of the apartment building, he pinched me on the behind and gave me a quick peck on the lips. He walked me up to the door and delivered me to Jay.
Jay thanked him for bringing me home and Roger left with the helpful rigger.
The door shut behind me as my rescuers left to return to the party and all hell broke loose.
"I was on the balcony when you two came in!" he had bellowed at me.
"There was only one persons head in the car and you were giving him head weren't you?"
"Jay you are delusional, they gave me a lift home, that's all." I retaliated.
"Bullshit!" He yelled at me. "I knew that son of bitch wanted in your pants the first time I laid eyes on him!"
"Jay, there is nothing going on between us," I yelled back at him.
Jay may have had more of a clue than I had about the lift operator's feelings for me given his behavior when we arrived, but that did not constitute any

misconduct. Roger had done nothing unforgivable and certainly I had not been performing oral sex on him.
"Jay did it ever occur to you that I might have just had my head down because I was laying down on the seat, I am buzzed!" I had defended myself
"No fucking way." He spitefully accused me again.
"Jay you're screwed in the head!" I said, and I left to him to his delusions of my infidelity.
He wasn't satisfied though and he continued to bombard me with accusations, rough me up a bit, until he had awakened Emily.
The following morning when I woke everything was fine of course. Who would have known that there had ever been a conflict the previous night?

One night shortly after, Jay went out on a binge of his own while I was at home with Emily, and when he got home he was a wild man.
"I can get a girlfriend too." He had snarled at me. "I met her tonight."
He had a name for her and described her in detail for my benefit.
"I don't need you bitch." He bellowed and then removed his wedding band and threw it at me.
"Jay calm down." I said to him, "What in the hell is wrong with you?"
"Nothing bitch, nothing is wrong with me!" He retorted back to me.
"Jay you need to go to bed and sleep it off." I said as I attempted to guide him to the bedroom.
He complied with being led to the bedroom and then once inside the bedroom he grabbed me and shoved me to the bed. Jay was no light weight and I was powerless to fend him off. Unlike Kodie years before I was not successful in making an escape and I was raped by my own husband in my own bed in my own home.

After Jay passed out that night I retrieved the wedding band that he had thrown at me and laid it on the kitchen counter. I then removed my own band from my finger that had not been off since the day that he had placed it on my finger and I laid it beside his. This was the end in my heart. I knew that it was only a matter of time now. I was no longer prepared to even attempt to make a relationship work with him.

C. R. Perk

He awoke the following morning full of apologies as all abusers do and promising never to do it again. It carried no weight with me this time. I had been abandoned; but never abused, this was unacceptable.
I phoned into work and explained that I had issues at home right now and had to take the day off.

I don't know how they knew but they knew, and Jays name was mud at the marina from that day forward.

Chapter 21

Before Emily's first birthday, Jay and I moved with Emily to a less expensive duplex apartment in the neighboring town of Cape Coral. It did not offer the amenities that we had enjoyed at the more expensive complex apartment with a pool and tennis courts, but it was practical and after cleaning for two solid days it was fit to live in.
The drive for me to work was much longer and involved bridge tolls going to and from work but it was a lot less money and we mowed the lawn to help reduce our rent.

After the night that I had removed my wedding band I had no interest in maintaining a viable marriage with Jay and I was just hanging out for the time being because I doubted that I would be able to support myself and Emily on my income alone. Jay was still insecure about my involvement at work and he never got over the night of innocence when he wrongly accused Roger and me of misconduct. I exacerbated the situation by staying even later after work; which I could justify because I only sat in long toll lines immediately following a business day while everyone else was trying to get home too. So his anger only intensified and his fits became more frequent and more intense.

Then about two months before Emily's first birthday one of the managers at the marina was a having a birthday bash at the pub where we all frequented. There was a large group of marina personnel congregated to celebrate this birthday and ironically the only person that was not present was the birthday boy himself. This was of no consequence; we did not need a birthday to have good cause to party. We were blue collar hard working stiffs that seized every opportunity to socialize, relax and shoot the bull. So here we were having a birthday party with no birthday boy.

Once again I had too much to drink and this time I was not fifteen minutes from refuge but about forty minutes and Cape Coral is known for DUI arrests. I knew that I was at grave risk of getting into trouble, or harming myself or someone else if I attempted to drive home.

Amongst the party patrons was a technician that lived near by the pub and his nickname was Skippy. He was called Skippy because he was notorious for getting up to use the restroom and never coming back to the table. When he'd had enough he would not just say so and leave because he knew that he would be cajoled to have another so he would just slip away when no one was paying attention. There were many nights when Skippy had a beer bought for him by someone and he never returned to consume the beverage, so on this evening I decided to elicit Skippy in this practice.
"I think I am going to need to borrow your sofa." I had confided to Skippy in a quiet voice.
Skippy replied. "Ok no problem. When I tell you to, just get up and follow me out."
"Ok." I said with a secretive grin.
Skippy observed the situation and finally determined that it was time to make our move.
"Let's go now." He whispered to me.
We both got up and tried nonchalantly to make our secret escape. We exited the pub and began to walk towards Skippy's truck when suddenly I heard a command from Roger.
"Charlie, you're going with me." He shouted.
Skippy looked at me and I looked at Skippy, we each shrugged our shoulders.
I approached Roger and asked him where we were going.
"We're going to race J.D., get in" he said.
And for no reason that I can fathom to this day I did as I was told.

Roger and I took off for a rural road with J.D. close behind us. We lined the vehicles up and soon both trucks lunged forward in an attempt to out run the other. It wasn't much of a race, Roger missed second gear and J.D. took the honors. There was no humiliating shut down of the trucks where J.D. got the opportunity to gloat. J.D. turned his truck around and drove home. Roger and I drove to the beach. This was to be the beginning of something wonderful.

Roger and I sat on the beach in his truck and he reached over and kissed me, then he kissed me again and again. He stroked my cheek and said to me, "You are so pretty." I thanked him and kissed him again and again.

"This is all you want." He said gingerly and we continued to act on our pent up feelings for one another.

He was seriously involved with another woman. Seriously involved because they had been together for seven years, owned a home together and had a son, but they were not married. I was obviously married, had an infant, owned nothing and was totally miserable. He too was unhappy in his relationship although no one could have known that unless they were intent upon watching his activities. He was almost never at home opting to go to the pub or stay at the marina after hours. We were both doing the same things to avoid our unhappy circumstances at our homes.

We did not jump right into bed together but actually nurtured the companionship that now went beyond friendship. We stole moments away and it was easy to do because we worked together. After hour we would hang out together at the marina. We would go to his shed that served as his small shop, and drink beer together. Sometimes we were alone but more often other personnel would join us. The owner of the marina came round infrequently but he referred to our circle of vehicles where we parked to drink after hours as a caravan. Roger was building a drag bike and I would help him with the mechanics in my limited capacity and I polished his pride and joy the rear wheel.

We thought we were pretty sly and no one knew but the operations manager caught on quickly. He asked the girls in the office, "So when did Roger and Charlie hook up?" The girls in the office knew because women share everything with other women but the girls were sworn to secrecy. Their mouths dropped open and one of them asked, "How did you find out?"
"It was easy," he said. "Roger is spending way too much time in this office."
So much for our well kept secret.
We had also been spotted by Skippy one night when Roger and I had set up a destination point. When I saw Roger he approached my car and kissed me through the window and right behind us in his truck was Skippy.
"Well look at you two." He had chided us.
Roger and I were surprised to have been caught but we deserved it since we were kissing in a bar parking lot across the street from our usual hang out.

So our secret was no longer a secret and the entire marina knew about us. We only generated additional gossip to add to our little *'Peyton Place'. Everyone was doing some else's partner. It was a nutty time for those of us in our thirties that worked at the marina. Perhaps we were afraid that life was going to get away from us. Both of the girls in the office that worked under me were sleeping with two different technicians although only one of the girls was married. The operations manager was sleeping with one of the girls in the business office and she worked under the matriarch of the marina, who was also the wife of the operations manager. These two women worked together all day in the same office and then the three of them went out socially together after hours. This worked out well for them until the matriarch figured out that she was socializing with the girl that was sleeping with her husband. It was a time of secrecy and deception. Everyone knew who was sleeping with who accept the other person in each relationship. It was a delicious time in history for those of us that were caught up in our seedy little lies and illicit affairs.

Roger and I were once sitting in his truck at a location at the marina called 'the point'.
It was the farthest extremity on the property and there were only a few wet slips, blocked boats on land, and the fuel dock that was now closed for the day. One of the youngest and still naïve mechanics was out there fishing off the dock when he hooked a large Snook. He came to the truck to display his trophy to us. The fish was a solid 38 inches long and it was a good catch but Snook was not in season so he had to throw it back.
After praising his catch, I said to him, "You do realize that Roger and I never saw that fish because we were never here, don't you?"
"What do you mean you were never here? You are sitting right there and you saw it!" He naively responded. We had to see it because no one was going to believe his fish story if we didn't say that we saw it.
"Yes we saw it, but since we were never here, we could not have really seen it. Do you understand me now?" I asked him.

*4

He looked confused for a moment and then it suddenly dawned on him why we could not have seen his great catch. He simply blushed and went back to his fishing.

Roger and I went to lunch at the same time each day and we would take both cars, leave mine at a restaurant parking lot and I would ride with him to his home. It was there that we had our first intimate experience. Given that we only had an hour it was somewhat short and sweet, but definitely more sweet than short.
We were sharing secrets about our unhappy relationships with our significant others and it was then that he told me that he had known that Jay was and had been abusive for quite some time.
"That day that you called and said that you were not coming in I knew that something was wrong and then the next day you came in and your eyes were black." He said to me.

"He had beaten you and I knew it." He continued.
"He didn't actually beat me with his fists." I responded.
"Your eyes were black!" He reiterated.
They could not have been black due to a blow to the face because Jay had never struck me in the face, but they may have had dark circles under them due to the stress involved.

Roger was living his own hell with a woman that was a workaholic and never at home. The romance had left their relationship some time before and he was sticking it out because of the jointly owned home and his son. We agreed that we would never leave our significant others and we would never have a future together; we would only enjoy one another for as long as it lasted.

We had met in a public park one night and I had left my car as we always did and he and I went to the beach once more in his truck. This night was the most romantic setting with the palm trees blowing in the breeze, the full moon glowing above us, the water lapping the sand and not a soul in sight. We made love there beside the gulf and it was the most romantic experience I've ever had. After our love making we sat on the tail gate of the truck, drank beer and talked for hours. We were both very conscious about the environment since it was our livelihood and we threw all the empty beer cans into the floor board of the truck.

When we left the beach the floor board was covered with beer cans and neither one of us could move without the cans rattling. We drove back to the park where my car was parked and before either one of us knew what was happening we were surrounded by police cruisers.

"Oh shit!" Roger said, "This ain't good!"

"No shit!" was all that I could say.

As the officers approached the truck Roger advised me to say as little as possible.

Two police men approached each of our windows and they asked to see our ID's. I had to reach for my purse that was located on the floor board between my feet and amongst all those empty beer cans. As I reached for my purse all those cans began to clatter together and I knew that there was no way that the officer could not hear them.

"Wait here and stay in the truck." The officers ordered us.

Roger and I sat frozen in the truck, both of us thinking the same thing. 'This is going to be very hard to explain to our significant others when we get hauled downtown and booked together.'

While the officers were running our ID's I asked Roger what he thought was going on.

He didn't know either and once again instructed me to just be quiet.

It seemed like an eternity before the police officers returned to the truck and handed our ID's back to us.

"You can go." The officers said and then returned to their cruisers and left.

"What the hell was that all about?" I asked Roger.

"They were looking for a drug deal. They had to have been or they would never have let us go with all of these empty beer cans." Roger reasoned.

"Well thank God for that." I said with relief in my voice. Then I started to laugh and said to him, "The cops were looking for the bad guys and come upon a couple that are clearly sneaking around and having an affair. I bet despite their disappointment that they didn't get their bust that they are laughing their asses off right now."

"Yea, I bet they are too. Thank God they didn't search the truck. Forget the beer cans I'm packing a pistol under the seat." He replied.

"Oh, wonderful!" I said.

"Yea wonderful!" He reiterated

"Can you imagine how hard it would have been to explain to Jay and Glenna that we had been arrested together for illegal possession and consumption of alcohol with an additional charge for an illegal fire arm?" I said to him.
"We were really lucky," he said, "and the beer cans were the least of my worries."
We would in the future laugh about the near fall tragedy but for this night we were just relieved to have gotten out of the incident without arrest. We said our goodbyes and I returned to my car. He headed south to his home with Glenna and I headed north to my home with Jay.

To this day I don't know how I got away from Jay so frequently in the evenings and left him with Emily but it was increasing more and more and he was actually tolerating it. I found more and more excuses for going to the pub with my friends from the marina and I was there frequently. Jay and I quarreled a lot of the time and he did not understand why I was so intent to hang out with these people. His temper was explosive and it was nothing for him to throw food at me in the kitchen or to overturn furniture.

One weekend when Gabrielle and Seth were visiting we got into an argument and I wanted to remove the children form the scene so I loaded Emily into her car seat and commanded the other two children to get into the car. As I attempted to start the car and drive away, Jay jumped on the hood. This did not overly deter me; I would have driven away and thrown him from the hood except that before I could accomplish that he had kicked in the windshield. Seth had actually bonded with Jay because they would go fishing and do guy things together. Gabrielle never did warm to him and incidents like this did nothing to improve the situation. Seth actually had wanted to stay with Jay when this madness occurred that day but it was still very upsetting to him. Emily of course was oblivious; or was she?

On another occasion Jay shattered the driver's side window to one of our cars when I was in it attempting another escape. I was covered with broken glass however I was not injured due the safety factors that car builders use to make the glass shatter but not cut. These incidents always occurred when I was trying to get away from him. He would stop at nothing to prevent me from leaving him and his abusive temper.

Another night when we were at home together and an argument broke out between us; he picked me up wearing nothing but a pair of bikini underpants and attempted to carry me out the front door in an effort to throw me out. This time I surprised him and landed my foot against the wall beside the front door and I kicked off the wall with all my might. This sent both of us flying backwards and tumbling on to the floor. I quickly got up and ran to the bedroom where I locked myself in.

Our home was a constant combat zone and I spent more time and money cleaning up messes and making repairs than is even imaginable. Roger knew what was happening in my house but there was little he could do but threaten to shoot the son of a bitch. Thankfully it never came to that but it came close.

At the time that all of this madness was occurring at home and I was having an affair with Roger, my workdays at the marina were from Tuesday through Saturday and I took Mondays off. One Monday in June I took Emily to her babysitter and I went to the beach. Out of the blue Jay showed up at the beach. He was attempting to catch me doing something wrong but to his frustration all he caught me doing was lying in sun, listening to the radio and drinking beer totally alone. Soon after his arrival he decided that he wanted to go see this pub where I hang out with all of my marina buddies. So I packed up my cooler and beach towel, tossed a tank top over my suit and took him to the pub.

The pub was a dive, and nothing to write home about, but it is where I chose to socialize and hang out with my friends. If Jay wanted to see it, I saw no reason not to take him.

We sat in the pub for quite a while until it was time to go pick up Emily. I stopped on the way back to our apartment to pick her up and Jay went home ahead of me. Jay continued to drink.

When I arrived at the apartment with Emily, Jay was fully intoxicated and making spaghetti. Jay has few commendable attributes but he can cook and did so frequently.

Emily was fifteen months old now and able to eat most table foods so I prepared her for dinner and put her in her high chair.

Jay immediately began to rant about the pub and what a dive it was. He raged on and on about Roger and the crew that I hung out with and then eventually lost total control and began throwing food every where. I grabbed Emily from her high chair and he grabbed the chair and overturned it. He threw spaghetti on the ceiling, the floor and the walls and I left the apartment and attempted to put Emily in the car for another escape attempt. Once again he refused to let me in the car so I walked away from him and went to the neighbor's door. Our neighbors opened their door and I shoved Emily into their arms.
"Keep her for me please!" I said through my rage.

I began walking down the road going no where except away from Jay. Jay ran me down and literally hurled me over his shoulder then dropped me to the pavement. I landed hard and I was covered with road rash. Jay picked me up again and started to carry me back towards the apartment. I looked down the road and saw a boy on a bicycle.
"Little boy, little boy, go call the police!" I screamed at him.
The boy spun his bike around and started riding the other direction as Jay carried me back to the duplex apartment. Once back at the apartment after he had set me down again, I immediately went back to the neighbors to retrieve my daughter.
"Charlie, settle down." Jay yelled at me.
"Go to hell!" I yelled back at him.
Emily was back in my arms. I was wearing only the bikini and tank top that I had worn to the beach and I had blood running down my right hip, my back, my right hand, elbow and forearm. I prompted the neighbors to come look at my kitchen, but they were relatives of one of Jay's friends and chose not to get involved. I was standing out doors extremely shaken by the impact of the pavement and the level of abuse that Jay had just displayed when to my astonishment the police pulled up to the duplex.
'Oh my God, the boy had called the cops, thank you little boy who ever you are!' I thought to myself.
The police were not happy. The male officer went to Jay and the female officer came to me. She was a pretty young blonde hard headed female that had no tolerance for men that beat up on women. She wanted to take him to jail right there and then, but I refused to allow her to do that. If the same incident occurred now in Florida I could not have stopped that action

because in domestic battery cases someone is going to jail if the police are called.

"Don't take him to jail." I said, "Just get Emily and me out of here."

The male officer detained Jay while I went back in to the apartment to get Emily's diaper bag and a change of clothes for myself. The female officer accompanied me while I got mine and Emily's provisions and she was witness to the mess in the kitchen.

"If I have to come back here again he is going to jail!" she said to me. I knew that she was not kidding.

"I don't care just get us out of here now please." I pleaded.

Emily and I were loaded into the back seat of the police car and transported to the shelter for battered women. When we arrived at the shelter they took pictures of my injuries and then advised me of my rights and responsibilities. They showed me where my refrigerator space was located and showed me where Emily and I were to sleep. Apparently the women that are brought here stay for extended periods of time. I had no intention of making this my make shift long term home, but our short stay would turn out to be a very long night.

The shelter was in a secret location where the abusers could not find their victims and we were instructed not to reveal where we were although we were allowed to use the phone to communicate with others outside. It was equipped with a large living room and dining area and had several refrigerators for each of us to store our provisions. I was expected to help with cleaning and to go to work if I was able. I was instructed that alcohol was prohibited at the shelter, but if I had a drinking problem then arrangements could be made to prevent withdrawal. It was almost as if the sanctuary of safety was a training ground for women that have no sense of self reliance, which I guess some of them needed. I was not one of them and found it a bit insulting to my intelligence that the volunteer workers felt that they needed to assist me on the most fundamental tasks in caring for myself and my child.

I was shown to Emily's and my sleeping quarters that was a very small room equipped with beds. I had a room mate with three children so it was a bit crowded, but it was better than spending another night with Jay. Through out the entire night if Emily was sleeping then one of my room mates children were not and we were constantly interrupting one another's efforts to rest. I finally gave up on getting any rest in that room so I took Emily to the living room where we could sleep on the sofa. Then before dawn I was awakened by one of the staff and informed that it was not permitted for me to sleep on the sofa in the living area. So I picked Emily up once more and spent the remainder of the pre-dawn hours attempting to sleep with the three children that never slept all at the same time.

I got up early the following morning, before most of the other victims had even gotten out of bed and bathed myself and Emily. I knew that this was not going to work out for us, but I was enormously grateful for the rescue. So I packed up Emily, her diaper bag, my purse and all of our overnight provisions and left the shelter. Since I could not reveal the location of the shelter I carried Emily who was a chubby child that weighed in at about thirty five pounds in the sweltering Florida summer time heat for approximately two miles while also carrying all the things that I had grabbed the night before. I finally arrived at a filling station where I called a cab company to come pick us up.

The cab took us to the marina where I went immediately to my office. I had to tell everyone what had occurred the night before and where I had spent the night. I then ask the operations manager if Roger could take me to the Justice Center so that I could begin legal proceedings. Of course he agreed to my wishes.

Roger dropped me at the Justice Center about ten o'clock in the morning and then left to return to work. I told him I would phone the marina when I was ready to be picked up. So into the Justice Center I went and headed for the civil department.

Emily was a sweetheart infant and she endured the long day very well. I'm not sure how I managed to keep her fed but we somehow managed through the day. When I arrived at the civil court section of the Justice Center I was instructed to write down my cause for action. I asked the Courts for an Injunction for Protection and requested that Jay be evicted from the marital residence so that I could return to our home with our minor child. I was instructed to write on a separate sheet of paper everything that had occurred and I'm sure this was verified through the police department where a report was made.

By four o'clock on June twenty six the Judge had signed all the necessary paper work and I telephoned the marina to summons our pick up by Roger. Ironically this was Roger's birthday.

Roger picked us up and took us back to the marina. Emily and I went home with one of the girls from my office and we lived with her and her three children for about three days; until Jay had been served and forced to leave the marital residence. The girl that we stayed with was a very good friend and I had spent a good deal of time at her home during those very turbulent days. Fortunately I had never allowed Jay to know where she lived so I felt safe and secure in her double wide trailer which was located in such a remote area of North Fort Myers that I doubt that the FBI could have found me.

After the three days had passed and I learned that Jay had been evicted, Emily and I returned to the duplex apartment. The neighbors in the other side of the duplex absolutely hated me now so there was not much communication between them and me but that was alright. I was safe now.

I returned to work and returned Emily to her child care provider. Once again I attempted to get my life back on track. I contacted the land lord and got permission to pay my rent in two payments since I got paid on a bi-weekly basis and I continued to mow the lawn to reduce the rent. They were compassionate to my circumstances and agreed.

I was once sitting at my desk at work and crying because I did not have seventy five cents to pay the bridge toll to get back home. The operations manager came in and dropped a twenty dollar bill on the desk in front of me.

"I can't take that," I said to him, "that's the marinas money for that boat that you just lifted."

"No it's not," he said, "that's a tip from the customer."

I knew that he was lying but I needed the money too much to argue with him. The marina personnel were my family now and I could always count them.

The madness with Jay did not just go away. He had moved in with friends but he was constantly violating the restraining order. He once broke into the apartment to harass me and when I attempted to phone the police he jerked the phone from the wall and threw it into the yard. One night he watched Roger and me while were intimate through the bedroom window and then he called the police and told them that he needed to be escorted into the apartment to get something personal that he needed. It was very embarrassing because Roger attempted to hide and Jay found him huddled in a closet, but it was not illegal for me to entertain anyone in my home. Jay had a very hard time figuring out what he had so desperately needed that he had asked the police to escort him into the dwelling where he was court ordered not to be near. The policeman saw through his antics and ordered him out of the apartment.

Jay later went back to the pub where Roger and I hung out. I was not present that day but Roger and one of his best friends were. Roger's friend was equal to Jay in his height and weight so this would have been a fair fight if it had occurred.
Jay just sat and glared at the two men the entire time that he was there. Roger's friend had wanted to take him outside and give him an attitude adjustment.
Roger is a small man by contrast to Jay and he never goes to a gun fight with a knife. He knew that the odds were slim that he could actually over power Jay although the two of them most assuredly could have, however any conflict would not have stopped with Roger and his friend because this was Roger's turf and all of the other patrons would have joined in. This was a rough crowd, Harley riders, drug dealers, construction workers, all blue collar and all friends of Rogers. Had a conflict broke out Jay would have ended up in the emergency room at the very least. Wisely he left.

Glenna is not a stupid woman and I am sure that she suspected that Roger was seeing someone, she may have even suspected that it was me, I don't know. But eventually Roger screwed up. He and some of his friends were going to the sprint races in a town about thirty miles north of Ft. Myers and my girl friends and I drove up to the join them. We smuggled beer into the stands and drank through the entire event. When the races ended we drove both vehicles back to Ft. Myers where we stopped at a bar that my girl friend liked to frequent and we continued to drink. At this time Roger had a passion for tequila and started doing shots of Quervo. At the close of the evening Roger was so intoxicated that he was beyond reasoning with. He refused to get into the truck that he had ridden up in and insisted that he wanted to go with me. Not knowing what else to do with him I took him home with me and he crashed in my bed. The following morning I tried repeatedly to get him up so that he could return to Skippy's and tell Glenna that he had stayed there because he was so intoxicated the night before but he would not get up. When I finally got him up and had dropped him off at Skippy's it was eleven o'clock in the morning so he didn't even get home until noon. By that time Glenna had already contacted the people that he should have been with and he was mysteriously missing in action. When he finally staggered up to his home, Glenna was packing his truck and moving him out. To what extent he had been busted is unclear but she was justifiably fed up and he was leaving.

I tried to get him to come to my apartment but he hated Cape Coral and chose instead to sleep in his truck at the marina. It was really quite amazing how quickly he found an apartment though and soon he had created his own residence with the minimal provisions that Glenna had given him.
It was very hard for Roger when his son realized that daddy was moving out and Roger came to his new apartment with tears in his eyes the day that he told his son good-bye. It broke my heart for him and his son and I felt responsible. Roger was quick to assure me that it was only a matter of time and that I should not feel that way.
"If it hadn't been you," he said, "it would have been someone else."

It was now common knowledge that Roger and I were romantically involved and we freely and openly displayed our affection for one another. Glenna was much more responsible and did not retaliate and attempt to make us miserable; the same cannot be said for Jay.

Roger was once at the marina hooking up with a man from Maine who had live Maine lobster that he was giving away. I was at Roger's apartment waiting with kettles warming, and administering a nebulizer treatment to Emily who was having another episode with her asthma. She was sitting on the kitchen counter top as I gave her the breathing treatment and the front windows began to rattle. Then the side door was being pounded and the locked door handle rattled. I shut down the machine and sat Emily on the floor and then went to investigate what all the noise was about. I could not believe it. Since he could not find us at the apartment in Cape Coral he had actually learned where Roger now lived. I went to the door and told him to leave and of course he refused. He was drunk again and demanding that I open the damn door.

"I am not opening this door!" I shouted at him through the locked door.

He then went back to the front windows and was pounding them so hard that I thought he would break one. I went back to the door that I opened only a jar and screamed for him to get the hell out of here. He ran to the door and attempted to break entry but I was actually able to prevent this from happening and before he could attempt another break in Roger drove up. When Roger arrived; Jay fled on foot to where ever his car was parked.

It was like that all of the time for a very long time. These conflicts always occurred when Emily was with me, because that was when he was free to get drunk. Every time he created havoc in my life, Emily was there and she suffered too.

Eventually Jay found an efficiency to live in and I allowed him to take Emily for weekend visitations. He had abused me not Emily, so I saw no reason that I should not allow him to have her for short periods of time.

When my lease became due my landlord informed that he had sold the duplex that I was living in and he doubted that the new owners would be willing to allow me to continue renting on a bi-weekly basis. It was also more than probable that the rent would be increased. So I began to look for a new place for Emily and me to live. I found a spot on a major road in Cape Coral, signed the lease and picked up the key. I then solicited the help of my co-workers to help me move and we loaded truck after truck with furniture and boxes. The entourage arrived at the street front apartment and Roger went ballistic,

"You can't move in here!" He said "What the hell are you thinking?"

"I have to have a place to live." I responded.

'Well this is stupid. You have a toddler and you are going to live in an apartment on this street? I don't think so, she'll get run over." He had ranted at me.

He then went in to pick the apartment apart and started with the inadequate lock on the front door and went on from there.

He exited the apartment and shouted to the movers, "She is not moving in here! Take all this stuff to the marina and we'll put in storage!"

And that is what we did. Fortunately there was in fact a storage facility adjacent to the marina property and we loaded everything into one large storage unit.

The following day I returned to the woman that had rented me the apartment and I attempted to explain to her that my boy friend did approve of the apartment because he felt it was unsafe for my daughter to live on that busy street. She could have been unyielding because I had signed the lease, but to my astonishment she conceded and let me out of the contract.

Now with no where else to go with my child, I moved in with Roger for a brief period of time. There was in fact absolutely nothing wrong with the apartment on the busy street and Emily was simply his excuse. The truth is that Roger did not want me to continue to live in Cape Coral because he did not want to deal with the bridge tolls. It was too far for him to protect me from Jay and he hated the town to begin with. So I moved in with him for a short period of time while I looked for a place more to his liking. In time I found a run down complex that the new owner was slowly remodeling unit by unit. It was on a secondary street so that Emily was safe from traffic and Roger could walk to my apartment from his. When I entered the apartment still under going face lift construction I rented it.

The new owner kept trying to sell me the apartment telling me what he was going to do to continue improvements.

"I know that you will do it justice." I had said to him. "I want it."

I gave him a deposit and waited for completion.

It was my sanctuary. It had a living room, a kitchen a bedroom and bathroom with only a stand up shower. The entire apartment had seven jealousy windows that covered nearly every wall with hard wood floors through out. There was a sink, stove, and a small refrigerator but no disposal or dishwasher. Limited cabinetry in the kitchen a very small air conditioner mounted in the living room. I was in love with it. I was minutes from the marina, beach, grocery and Roger and it was affordable. Emily and I were very content here but it was here that Emily began to show her first signs of anger.

Through the Eyes of Betsy McCall

The lady next door was a sweetheart with learning disabilities, but she went to work everyday on a bicycle. She was the most determined and functional person I had ever known with the extent of her disabilities. When she went to the grocery, work or laundry mat she rode a bicycle pulling a cart behind her and she sported a flag over her bike so that motorists would see her. Many people made fun of her but it was so unjust. She had help from no one and she had every strike against her but she never gave up. Rain or shine she road to and from her job where she did laundry for a large vacation resort that was approximately ten miles away.

Her name was Angie and she could hear Emily when she was having one of her fits. I attributed Emily's fits to the terrible twos, but Angie would come over and tell her to stop her fits. She would almost lecture Emily to behave for her mother.

Angie shared with me that she knew that she was 'not smart' like other people and I found that to be an amazing thing for her to share with me. She also told me that she had a sister that was 'smart', but she never came around. Angie was on her own and doing well.
People would make fun of her as she rode her bicycle up and down the streets with her orange flag waving over her head, but I felt that it was cruel for them to do that. Angie displayed greater strengths than a lot of 'smart' people I know have. In a strange way she became a friend to me and I respected her for her courage and her caring for other people.
She was an amazing woman given her disabilities.

Then Jay started to come around and this really upset Angie. She did not like him and that was all there was to it. She actually became my watch dog and she watched for his unwanted visits because they always erupted into arguments. He was no longer able to control me and still under a restraining order, so the abuse had stopped but we were always arguing when he came around. This upset Angie terribly. She was dedicated to me and my effort to raise a child with limited income and provisions. I also think that she saw things with the same limitations that her mind processed information. She had limited mental capacities and there for she saw every situation with the same limitations. It was black or white, good or bad, or like or dislike. She actually yelled at Jay on occasion and told him to go away and leave us alone. She would tell me if he had come around when I was not there and she was in reality the ideal neighbor and I liked her very much.

One day she shared with me that she was having fun with a man 'between the sheets'; that was her definition of having a sexual relationship. I never saw the man that she was involved with but he was the Captain of a recreational vessel that did day cruises from the vacation resort where she did laundry each day. She told me that his name was Captain John. I question the truth in this when she first shared it with me because I never saw the man and she said that he was coming to her apartment. However she continued to share these experiences with me and after a while I realized that it had to be true.

Captain John was arriving in the very late hours or early dawn and gone before I awoke in the morning. Angie would become annoyed with Captain John because he was not readily available when she might need a favor or a ride, but he came around for the 'between the sheets' episodes at his own discretion.

It was quite by accident that I met Captain John at a water front bar and restaurant on the beach where all the marine industry personnel congregate on Sunday nights. He introduced himself to me and proudly announced that he was the Captain of the 'Miss Mary Excursion' day cruise ship. This was Angie's 'between the sheets' partner and I suddenly knew what the fat bastard was doing. He was what Angie would call 'smart' and of normal intelligence. He was using Angie to satisfy himself sexually but hiding his activities from the rest of the world.

"So, Captain John," I asked him, "how are things going between you and Angie?"

"What are you talking about?" he asked me with guilt written all over his face.

"You know what I'm talking about." I responded and left it at that. I wanted him to know that that I was on to him and his pitiful misuse of Angie.

Soon after that Angie told me that he had stopped coming around and she didn't understand it. I never told her what had happened between Captain John and me because I did not want to tell her that she was being used by a sick individual who was taking advantage of her disability. She was disappointed but I knew in time that she would move forward again.

Through the Eyes of Betsy McCall

I only stayed in my sanctuary for a year and inside of that year Gabrielle and Seth were picked up every other weekend for visitations and returned on Sundays. While they were visiting one weekend Jay showed up once again and began to create a conflict with me.

"Jay, I have had it with you. Now get the hell out of my apartment!" I had shouted at him.

Jay never had the courtesy to leave when I asked him to. He continued to make accusations and argue with me still intent upon laying blame. Although legally we were still married he had no control over me and this made him even angrier.

"Jay, get the hell out of this apartment and leave us alone, please!" I ranted at him again.

He wasn't leaving and he became more and more belligerent, cussing and telling me and my children what a bitch I was.

"Jay you are only upsetting the kids! Now get out of here." I shouted at him.

"Fuck you bitch. You've got these kids in here and you are screwing Roger right under their noses. Aren't you a wonderful example for them!" he had shouted back at me.

"Jay you don't have a clue, we are not the irresponsible idiots that you are, now get out of here now!" I shouted at the top of lungs.

He continued to rant and cuss and I continued to yell back for him to just get the hell out of my home and then suddenly it all ended. Seth who had always felt close to Jay had reached his limit and at long last had found his loyalty. "Jay just get out of here!" he cried out as tears streamed down his little face. "You are making my mom crazy, just go away!" He wailed as he held his hands over his face and cried hysterically.

I went to my son and held him in my arms to comfort him.

"Are you satisfied now?" I asked Jay sarcastically.

Jay looked ridiculous after being challenged and humiliated by a seven year old child. He had finally met his match and he quickly left at the request of my son.

Chapter 22

When my lease became due it was the end of my time in my sanctuary. Roger and I were never apart and if he was not at my apartment then I was at his.

"This is stupid." He had said to me. "Between us we are paying in rent what we could be paying for a mortgage payment. Why don't you just move in with me?"

So it wasn't long before Emily and I had moved into Roger's apartment and we were splitting the expenses. I was still legally married to Jay and in no big hurry to get a divorce. I had sworn to God that if he just got me out of that mess that I would never get married again. So I felt no urgency to terminate the legal ties. Roger did not see it that way but he really didn't insist on a daily basis that I follow through with a legal divorce. So I lived with Roger for two more years before Jay and I were actually divorced. In reality I was separated from Jay and still legally married to him longer than I had lived with him as a married couple. Roger had told me early on that he was never going to marry again having failed in a marriage prior to his relationship with Glenna, so I didn't see any reason to divorce Jay because he was not stopping me from doing anything that I wanted to do anyway.

Roger had also told me one night in his truck early on that I should listen to a song on the radio. The song on the radio was *"Freebird" performed by Lynyrd Skynyrd and basically served to inform me that Roger would never be tied down again. I took the song to heart.

Roger and I shared everything and went everywhere together. He was actively racing a drag bike and we spent every dime that we made on racing. He was the rider, I was his starter and I towed him from the trailer to the pits before he made a pass. These events were a very big deal and he spent the days before an event getting the bike ready and I bought our food, ice and drinks for the track. The night before we left we loaded the U-haul trailer with leathers, gloves, boots, helmet, a generator, air tank, a starter cart and batteries, a moped, tools and ultimately the six hundred pound bike itself. Our tow vehicle was loaded with our clothes, groceries, coolers, coffee pot, and what ever else I thought we could possibly need. More often than not there were two drag bikes in the U-haul because our friend Bill went with us and also competed. Often the events were miles from our home and we would travel as far as Atlanta and Indianapolis to participate in the races. It was very cramped in a pick up truck and a small extra cab but these were the golden years despite set backs such as blown motors, slipped chains, broken sprockets, and worn out slicks. We pulled a six by eight U-Haul to these events and actually called ourselves 'U-Haul' racing. We found the cleanest and cheapest hotels to stay in and repeated our visits to the same facilities if they had been acceptable in the past. We were having the time of our lives and we packed the kids along when ever possible. Racing became our family sport.

So Roger and I worked together at the marina during the week and raced together on the weekends. When we weren't racing, we were boating, and when we weren't boating we were socializing at one drinking establishment or another. Roger and I were inseparable and I had outsiders actually tell me that they envied our relationship.

Early on in our relationship I had learned of Roger's heart condition. I knew nothing about the workings of the heart but I could hear the clicking in his chest. He explained to me that he had a prosthetic aortic valve because he had been born with a leaky valve.

When he was seven the surgeons repaired the valve and then when he was fourteen, they went back in and replaced his defective valve with a mechanical one. He explained to me that it is a ping pong ball in a cage and when his heart pumped it forced the ball to move forward and then the ball would come back and stop the flow of blood with each beat of his heart. He also told me that he was not expected to live to be thirty years old at the time that the valve was put in. Although this frightened me very much he had already proven them wrong and I decided that I loved him enough to risk it. Roger and I were both thirty three years old at that time.

A customer at the marina who is to this day a friend was also in pharmaceutical sales.

When I spoke to him about Roger's heart valve and discussed the medications that he was taking on a daily basis the salesman asked about his coumadin intake. Roger came in to the office and heard us talking about him and smiled at George, and said, "Well go ahead and tell her the rest. If I fall off the bike and sustain a head injury, I'll bleed to death."

Alarmed I looked at George for verification. George concurred that he very well could bleed to death if he sustained serious injury because his blood is so much thinner than the rest of our blood and what someone else might survive, he probably would not. This was not terribly comforting. I soon learned that in order for Roger to survive he had to take the drug for the valve to work properly. The drug in larger doses is used in rat poison. When the rat takes the bait, it hemorrhages internally which consequently results in death. In Roger's case, it's as important that his blood be thin as it is for a car to operate with motor oil. I also learned that alcohol increases the risk and further thins the blood and makes the medication harder for the health care providers to monitor the level of coumadin needed.

For a couple of years we went through all the motions of living together happily and I even divorced Jay in 1993. Emily was in childcare right around the corner from our apartment and we continued to both work at our jobs at the marina.

Then one day Roger fell ill while I was waiting for him to come to the office and go to lunch together as we did every day. I was growing impatient because he was about fifteen minutes late when he was found by another co- worker wandering around the work yard dazed and bleeding from his forehead. He was confused and didn't know where he was, or what time it was, or what day of the week it was.

My boss said, "Charlie, get him to a hospital, now!"

I got him into my car and headed for the nearest hospital. I didn't even know exactly how to get to the hospital but I headed in that general direction. As I headed south on the road in front of the marina, Roger said to me, "Charlie don't take to me to the hospital. If you take me to the hospital, I'm gonna kick your ass! Just take me home."

I quickly turned the car around and headed for home. Suddenly he began to clutch his chest, wailing and wreathing in pain.

"Screw you big boy, you are going to the hospital!" I shouted at him.

I turned the car around and headed south again. He continued to rant at me not to do this between chest spasms and wreathing pain but I was not listening anymore.

I was terrified and I kept driving in what I knew was the general direction of the hospital.

I came to a major intersection and rolled my window down and asked for directions to the hospital. The other motorist said that I needed to turn at this intersection; it was down the road on the right. I threw the car into reverse and backed the car so that I could get into the turn lane and then turned onto the road with out regard for traffic lights or other motorists.

Roger was still clutching his chest and wreathing around all over the front seat. I finally found the hospital and drove into the emergency room entrance where the ambulances come into the hospital emergency room.

"Mam, you can't use this entrance this is just for….." an attendant attempted to advise me.

"Get this man in there, he is a heart patient and he is having excruciating chest pain. I'll move the fucking car just get him in there!" I screamed at the emergency room attendant.

Everyone responded to my commands as if I was in charge.

Once Roger had been taken to the emergency room and placed on a gurney, I moved the car as I had promised. I sat vigil by his gurney where he continued to wreath and I came to realize at last that he was delirious and really had no sense of what was going on or what he was saying.

The emergency room nurses drew blood on him as I answered all their questions about what had occurred, in as much as I was able to provide that information. Pretty soon the nurses came back and said something about having drawn a purple bullet and the attending emergency room physician did not believe the results. They did another draw of Roger's blood, and then a third. After three draws they were satisfied that they were not getting false results and immediately put an I.V. of blood on him. He was then taken to a room where I sat with him until I had to leave to go home, due to my own fatigue and there being no place for me to sleep.

I have sense asked medical personnel what a purple bullet is and it is not a medical term, but probably something that this particular group of people used in their daily work to explain an unbelievable blood draw. In Roger's case he was five units low on blood. There are thirteen pints of blood in the human body and Roger was running on only eight pints.

I walked into his hospital room the following morning and he looked like he had been to the beach. The color that had so slowly faded away that I did not even notice since his blood loss was gradual was now back. He had nearly bled to death before my very eyes. We all thought that he had collapsed at work due to the loss of blood, but the hospital was not releasing him because they needed to know where the blood loss had occurred. He was poked, prodded, scanned, scoped and x-rayed until there was nothing left for the healthcare professionals to diagnose from his mouth to his rectum.
The final findings were that he had been bleeding excessively from his rectum do to hemorrhoids for a very long time and he had ignored them and never sought professional help. That was the good news.
The only day that I was not there to speak to the physician and ask questions was the day that the thoracic surgeons went to his room to speak to him.
When I arrived, the smile was gone and he was not so excited to see me.
What had happened since I had left him the day before? He looked wonderful when I left him and I was hopeful that he would be released soon.
I tried to be cheerful and bring his spirits up but it was futile.
"Ok, what's wrong?" I finally asked him.
"The thoracic guys came into see me." He said.
I had no idea who the thoracic guys were so I asked him who they are.
"They are the slice and dice guys." He responded sarcastically. "They want to open me up again."
"What happened, why?" I asked him gravely concerned and feeling a bit frightened.
"While they were looking for bleeding they decided to take a look at my valve and found an aneurism on my aorta beside the valve." He said.
I was visibly shaken by this finding but I also had enormous confidence in the technology now available and the skill of the surgeons. I had been raised by people in the medical field and I believed that everything was repairable.
Roger also knew that surgery was his only option but he refused to consider it. The aneurism was not large enough to cause serious consideration for an emanate burst, although it was inevitable that it would become larger.

Since Roger refused the advice of the surgeons he was finally released after a week of tests.

I couldn't really blame him; he was thirty five years old and did not want to go through another open heart surgery. He had vivid memories of the cough that was required of the patient following the invasive surgery; he remembered the pain of having his chest filleted the drainage tubes that were unsympathetically jerked from his abdomen and groin and he just did not want to endure the procedure again. I had never experienced anything like this, so I could only imagine. I made my pleas for him to reconsider but his mind was made up. I took him home and lived in fear that I would one day awaken beside a dead man.

It wasn't long after his release from the hospital that he collapsed again at the marina. This time an ambulance was called and he was once again transported to the hospital and this time I rode in the front of the ambulance as we transported him. There was a brief accident on the street in front of us and the paramedic driving the ambulance radioed the police to inform them of the fender bender caused by our quest to get through the traffic.

This collapse at the marina was witnessed by everyone, and it was clear this time that Roger had suffered a seizure. He had convulsed violently, ground his teeth and frothed at the mouth. When we arrived at the hospital he was once again admitted and test after test after test was performed to determine what had caused the seizure. Once again his chest and back muscles hurt him horribly, and this time I realized that the first trip to the hospital had also been a seizure. The convulsions are so strong that every muscle in the body are clinched and strained to their maximum potential. The contractions are so extreme that the muscles ache with excruciating pain following the seizure. After scanning his brain a thousand times and finding no other solution it was determined that he was having seizures due to alcohol withdrawal. I found this to be a ludicrous diagnosis and an excuse because the doctors had no better theory.

Roger now had a primary physician, a cardiologist, a thoracic surgeon standing by, and a neurologist. We left the hospital with that diagnosis and we both stopped drinking. I did so to give him the support that he needed to follow the physician's instructions, despite my belief that it was incorrect and unsubstantiated.

Since I did not really believe the neurologists findings I went to the library to research seizures and their causes. I learned there were several different types of seizures and they are caused by a number of stimulus' but what the medical professionals don't reveal is that they too have very little understanding of what prompt or substantiate the onset of seizures. Alcohol withdrawal however is indeed a trigger for grand mall seizures.

We followed the doctor's orders and gave up alcoholic beverages and still another seizure occurred although thankfully not at the marina. Each time that a seizure occurred, I would phone the paramedics and an ambulance would be dispatched. Eventually I became complacent about them. I knew that they could be life threatening, I knew that he could bite his tongue off but I also knew that they would transport him to the hospital and release him without any more understanding than we had with the first occurrence.

I think Roger suffered four seizures in the following year and miraculously the marina had only witnessed the one when the ambulance was summonsed. He was terrified that he would lose his job if the marina knew how frequently that they actually occurred and amazingly we managed to keep the frequency from our employer.

Then he came home for lunch one day from the marina and asked me to take the moped from him that he had ridden to work that morning. I was totally confused by this because this was a man that rode a six hundred pound drag bike at speeds in excess of one hundred forty five miles per hour, and he was asking me to take control of our baby tow bike. He left the running moped in my care. I turned the bike off, put it on its stand, and followed him into the house. He was lying on the sofa and having a full blown grand mall seizure.
I stood there and looked at him for a moment and hesitated to call the paramedics once more, but then I thought to myself, 'You've no idea what to do and he could die!'
So once again I dialed 911.
The ambulance personnel arrived and I answered all of their questions, His social security number is 301- 58-.....

He takes coumadin, and lanoxin, as I handed them the pill bottle so that they could verify the dosages.
His name, his age, etc., and then I asked the paramedics, "Can you tell that I've done this before?"
They grinned and concurred that I seemed pretty well rehearsed.

Eventually he was transported to the hospital once more. This was becoming common place so this time I did not ride in the ambulance but told the paramedics that I would follow in my car.

When I arrived at the hospital he was still in the emergency room and I told the attending nurse, "I do not want him admitted again. Just get him stabilized and I'll take him home."
"Who are you?" she asked me with obvious contempt for my arrogance.
"I'm his girlfriend and every time this happens he is admitted and nothing is ever found."
"Mam, you have no say in this. You are only his girlfriend." She had flatly stated.
I was a hell of a lot more than just a girl friend. I had never missed a doctor appointment with him since this night mare began, I had sat vigil at his bedside for days on end and I had been through entirely too many ambulance rides. Who did this bitch think she was?

The attending nurse or emergency room physician contacted Roger's primary physician and he advised them to grant my wish. He instructed them to stabilize him and send him home with me but he had better be in his office the following Monday.

The following Monday I entered the exam room with Roger as I always did by now and waited for the young physician to come in.
The usually lenient and upbeat physician was not so pacifist this trip.
"How are you feeling?" he asked Roger.
"I'm ok," Roger responded.
"Well I'm not." The doctor retorted. He was fighting a horrible head cold and felt really bad. It was pretty obvious. His next question was directed at me.
"What was he doing when this happened this time?" he asked me.

I told him of the incident with the moped that Roger had ridden to work that morning and that he had just arrived home when he handed me the bike and then went into the house and the seizure occurred.

He was not in the mood to coddle Roger this time. He had signed his medical release so that Roger could maintain his racers license despite the grave risks involved but this time he was not bending his own conscious moral medical ethics any more.

He looked square at Roger and without so much as a blink he said to him without reservation, "Do you know that if you'd had that seizure on that moped and you had torn that aneurysm that you would be sixty seconds to DOA. I don't care if I am there and all of my colleagues and surgeons are there; there is nothing that any of us could do. You would bleed to death in less than a minute. Have I made myself clear?" He asked sternly.

Roger nodded his head that he understood.

"You need to call the thoracic group and get this surgery scheduled as soon as possible." The doctor finished.

Roger had heard his doctor this time.

We left the doctors office and went to have lunch. I sat across the table from Roger as we awaited our food and I finally found the nerve to speak to him.

"So what are you going to do?" I asked him.

"I don't know, just shut up and leave me alone!" he barked at me.

I did not say another word to him about it for the remainder of the day. It was Valentines Day and not a very happy one.

The following morning when he awoke he had not even gotten out of bed yet when he rolled over and hugged me, "Call the surgeon. Let's get this shit over with."

For eleven months I had lived in fear that the aneurysm would burst and I would awake beside a dead man. At long last he had agreed to the surgery. I was on the phone by seven thirty and we had an appointment scheduled to meet with his surgeon.

The surgeon informed us that he had the newest and greatest prosthetic valve on the market and he was going to replace the old ping pong ball in a cage with this wonderful flapper that is made of the same material that

Apollo 13 was made of. This was interesting and I said to Roger, "Isn't it comforting to know that if you internally combust that your new valve will withstand the heat."

Admittedly this was sick humor but sometimes necessary to get though such emotionally challenging situations. Thoracic surgeons are a strange breed to begin with. They are no different than your auto mechanic when you have your car repaired. The mechanic does not care what color your car is when he is installing a water pump or a carburetor and a surgeon is much the same. He has internal work to do and every body is built pretty much the same and he has to put it in to proper running order. That day our surgeon was sharing with us the most up to date part that he would use when he repaired Roger's heart. If the surgeon appeared to a bit strange, Roger requested that we be allowed to bring his old ping pong ball in a cage home with us when we left the hospital.

The night before the surgery we sat outside the duplex apartment on the front porch and Emily played on her jungle gym that I had designed and Jay had constructed from un-unused sprinkler pipe. Roger's best friend and co-racer was also with us to provide moral support.

His support was a bottle of Quervo. Emily was playing on her jungle gym that we could not keep her off of and a neighbor's dog showed up from no where. Suddenly Emily came crying to us and said that the dog had bitten her on the thigh. This was all that Roger needed. All the pent up apprehension came crashing out of him and he was ready to kill a dog. It took some time and research to learn what dwelling the dog had come from but we found it. The pound was called and eventually the dog was apprehended. The owners had no record of immunization so the dog was eventually put down and checked for rabies. Fortunately there were no ramifications to the dog bite, but the deterrent in a strange way helped to alleviate some of the tension we were all attempting to deal with. Later in the evening, Roger's friend Bill brought the tequila out and began to administer shots to Roger. At first I did not dispute this but after a couple of shots, I lost my temper and called Bill aside.

"What are you doing?" I had ranted at Bill. "Tomorrow morning he is going under the knife to have life threatening surgery. He is also a bleeder and the last thing that he needs right now is to have his blood to thin and go into that operating room."

Already buzzed himself Bill responded to me feeling a bit unfairly charged, "Yea, but he is also scared shitless and this will help him to not concentrate so much on the operation."
Bill and I continued to argue but in the end I lost. We both loved the man and we both had the same fears. He continued to drink with Roger and I continued to be fearful.

The following morning I had to have Roger at the hospital at five thirty in the morning.
I drove in the dark morning hours to the hospital. As we approached the hospital he blurted out to me, "I changed my mind."
"Me too," was all I could say but I continued the drive to the hospital.
We were instructed on what floor we were to go to and then instructed to wait in a waiting room until the prep team came out to get him. We sat side by side and held hands as both of our apprehensions were mounting.
Eventually they came for him and he rose to follow them. He turned, looked back at me and then gave me a kiss. I saw fear in his eyes and it consumed me. I watched him walk away and all I wanted to do was to go get him, pull him back and take him back home, but I knew that I could not do that.

The surgery was scheduled to last four hours. I settled in for the long wait then I got up and moved about the hospital, I went to get a cup of coffee, go smoke a cigarette then return to the waiting area again. I spoke to a young woman whose father was also having heart surgery and we shared our stories. Then I got up and pranced some more.
Four hours came and went, then it was four and a half, then it was five. I went to the volunteer attendant and asked her to check on Roger and see how much longer it would be. She went to the OR and was told it would be about another twenty minutes. I sat with anticipation awaiting the face of the surgeon to appear to tell me everything was fine. I waited and I waited and I waited but the surgeon did not appear. Suddenly I heard all hell break loose on the other side of the wall where I sat waiting. I heard trays and medical staff crashing about in an obvious code blue situation.
Roger had coded, I was sure of it. I had pressured him to have this surgery and now he was not coming out of the anesthesia. I knew that he was to be packed in ice to thicken his blood and then technically terminated for the surgery. When the surgery was completed he did not respond when his heart

was prompted to resume beating. He was dead and I believed it. I began to pace and cry. The four hour surgery had gone far beyond that, the twenty minutes was exhausted and we were now working on six hours.

I went to the phone and called Bill's office. He wasn't there and his sales associate said that he thought he was on his way to the hospital.

"He had damn well better be," I said, "because I don't think I can do this alone much longer."

I hung up the phone and went to the restroom. When I returned the volunteer worker had became concerned and began to look for me. She knew that I was coming apart at the seams. The tears were streaming down my face but I was otherwise maintaining.

At six and one half hours I was standing in the hall when the surgeon came out of the operating room. As he approached me I noticed that he had Roger's blood in his ear.

He had no more than informed me that everything was fine and that Roger had been sent to recovery than the elevator door opened and Bill stepped out. If Bill had arrived thirty seconds earlier before the surgeon came out, I would have been sent to the psych ward because of the pent up hysterics that had built up inside of me. Everything would have come crashing out of me all at once.

I was told by the surgeon that I could see Roger in a couple of hours. I went to the sweet and kind volunteer that had so fretted about me and told her that this young man was going to take me out for a much needed beer and I would be back in a couple of hours.

We exchanged comforting hugs and Bill and I headed for a place to find a beer.

"You know Bill you have to wonder what type of person a thoracic surgeon really is." I had marveled to him. "What kind of person gets out of bed in the morning, showers, brushes his teeth, shaves, eats a bowl of cereal and then goes to work to saw other people's breast bones in half."

Bill concurred that it would take an unusual breed to choose that profession, "But thank God they do." He had concluded.

Truer words have never been spoken.

Two hours later we returned to the hospital and we were both allowed to go into the intensive care recovery unit. This was almost worse than the wait

had been. No one had prepared me for what I was about to see. Lying there in that bed was what used to be Roger. He was grey, his lips were blue, he had a tube in his mouth and a machine was breathing for him, there were tubes coming out of him everywhere and he was covered with tape and bandages. His mouth was abnormally distorted due to the tape and gauze that held the breathing tube in his mouth and if not for the machine that caused his chest to rise and fall I would have sworn that he was a corpse.
When I entered the intensive care unit I had felt elated. I ran into the young woman whose father was having surgery as well and she was crying.
"It will be alright," I had said to her as I scurried to see Roger.
It was not until after my elation had been destroyed by the sight of Roger's living corpse, that I realized that the bed that the young woman had been standing beside as she was crying had been empty. I suddenly realized that the code blue might not have been for Roger at all but for this woman's father. I felt terrible for her, but I did not see her again to express my sympathies and to correct my false reassurances.

I left the hospital and went home. There was nothing more that I could do for Roger right then and I did not want to see anymore of the horror that I just witnessed. When I arrived at our apartment I attempted to go to bed and rest. It had been a very long day and despite the fact that it was still day light I felt like I had been beaten up. I laid down on our water bed and every where I looked there were pictures of Roger and me. Roger on the boat, Roger on the drag bike, Roger at the air show, Roger and I in a bar laughing together, and I thought to myself, 'He will never be the same." I curled up into a ball and cried as I had never cried in my life. I cried until the exhaustion and emotional suffrage had beaten me and at long last I slept restlessly.

The following morning I returned to the hospital to see how the living corpse was doing.
They allowed me into the ICU and I almost wet my pants. Roger was awake, he was lucid and he was sitting in a chair drinking orange juice.
"Oh my God, look at you," I exclaimed. "You look wonderful!"
He may have looked wonderful compared to the previous day but he didn't feel all that wonderful. He knew that they had sawed his breast bone in two and he still had drainage tubes coming out of him, he was still on a

catheter and still in intensive care, but he was breathing on his own, alert, and alive!

It wasn't long before he was given his cough pillow that are made by the volunteers, and donated to the cardiac ward at the hospital. The pillow is designed to give the patient something to cradle against their filleted chest when they are instructed to cough to expectorate the remaining fluids in the lungs. They are given a breath flow meter to determine that their lungs are functioning adequately and then they are expected to take a walk. Roger's drainage tubes had been removed and he forced himself to cough despite the excruciating pain that accompanied this activity. On the third day following his surgery he was approached by yet another senior volunteer and told it was time to stroll down the hall. He was assisted from his hospital bed and then he took off like a rocket heading toward the hall..
The volunteer turned back to me and said. "Oh my, they must move faster when they are young."
I simply grinned at her; I knew that Roger was going to do what ever they wanted as quickly as possible to get a release from the hospital. He recovered quickly and was released on day five following the surgery.

Once he was at home he was unmanageable. The first thing he wanted to do was to have sex. This scared the hell out of me knowing that his heart rate would increase and I feared that he would blow out his sutures at the surgical sight on the heart valve itself.
He survived the act of intercourse and then refused to wear the socks that the hospital had sent home to prevent blood clots from forming in his legs. The next thing I knew he was upside in the trunk of my car wiring speakers. He would not be released to return to work for six weeks and he was going stir crazy. I could not keep him down and quiet.
Eventually he returned to the pub out of shear boredom. He came home from the pub one night and he had his last and final seizure.

I honestly thought at the time that he had drank too much and was ill from alcohol at first.
He was vomiting in our bed and talking out of his head.
"Roger what is wrong with you?" I had asked him in frustration.
"Your dad did it." He responded to me.

"My dad did what?" I asked him.
"Your dad did it!" he now shouted at me.
"What the hell did my dad do?" I shouted back.
Then he suddenly became frustrated and went to the bathroom where he continued to vomit. In his delirium he grabbed a towel rack and pulled it from the wall.

I got up and abandoned him. I wasn't going to sleep in a drunks vomit so I went to the sofa in the living room. The following morning I found him still lost and delirious, totally out of balance and unaware of where he was or what it was he was attempting to accomplish. Once more I called the paramedics who transported him to the hospital.
Once again he was diagnosed as a seizure patient and soon released.
I knew there were many differences between the grand mall seizures and what had occurred on this night and I was not satisfied with the diagnoses. I attempted to tell the attending medical personnel that he had not had the same type of seizure but no one wanted to listen to me.

Amazingly, the Governor of the state of Florida had just had an eschemic attack which was caused by a blood clot in the brain. The Governors symptoms were published in the news paper and his symptoms were identical to those that Roger had displayed. I went back to my library research and determined that Roger too had experienced a blood clot to the brain and his was probably the result of the recent surgery. Following the open heart surgery and the eschemic attack, there were no more seizures ever again.

Was the aneurysm interrupting the electrical impulses between the heart and the brain? I actually asked the surgeon this question to which he could not say for certain. He had never heard of such a thing. I still have no answers but I have my own theories. Why would the grand mall seizures cease after the aortic valve had been repaired?

Roger experienced a few scares in the months that followed because his seizures were always preceded by symptoms of dizziness and confusion, but they never resulted in anything more than anxiety. This occurred a few months later when I had left him to go to California to say good-bye to my mother.

Through the Eyes of Betsy McCall

Chapter 23

Mothers Day was approaching and our mother had basically been sent home to die. There were no more surgeries to be performed, no more chemo therapy treatments and no more radiation. She was staying alive through a feeding tube inserted in her stomach where she administered her own liquid nutrients. She weighed about ninety pounds and was provided all the liquid morphine she desired through Hope Hospice. Ellie and I knew that this would be our last chance to ever spend a Mothers Day with her so we agreed to fly to California for a Mothers Day celebration. Ellie arrived before I did as usual.

It was really a very nice reunion amongst women. Ellie had gotten our mother a very pretty night gown and robe and I had gotten her a cologne and powder ensemble. These were comfort gifts for a woman that had never received a Mothers Day gift and now had no future.

Mom insisted that we go to her bar where she could show off her children for the first time in many years. Ellie and I complied and it gave mom a lot of joy to show us off. I had recently had periodontal surgery and my teeth were very sensitive to cold so when I drank beer I did so through a straw. Ellie drank whiskey and water but she wanted an olive in her drink. The bar tender thought we were the strangest drinkers he had ever served. Mom was still attempting to drink her vodka but the bitter fluid burned her throat so she drank her vodka in a cup of warm water. She would tell the bar tender that there was too much vodka in the cup and have him pour some out and add more water. I soon lost favoritism with the bar owner.

"Mom, why are you paying for a full shot every time they make you a drink with warm water and a jigger of vodka?" I had asked her. "Why don't you order a shot and administer the vodka the way that you want it and have the bartender just fill your cup with warm water when you need it?"

My mother thought that I was a genius!

My mother also had more grit than John Wayne. She was in excruciating pain and taking syringes full of morphine in an effort to keep us entertained.

"Are you alright?" Ellie and I asked her repeatedly, "Do you need to go home and rest?"

"Are you in too much pain?"

"No" she lied, "I am fine."

She knew that this would be the last time that anything like this would ever occur in her remaining life time. She was not going to allow even the cancer to interrupt the joy that she was feeling as a result of Ellie and me being there for her.

At one point she took us to a picture of her now deceased husband and shared with us what the occasion was when the picture had been taken. It had been one of many festive occasions that they had spent together at the bar. I said to her. "Isn't it sad that we live half of our life before we finally find the right person to share our lives with?"

She readily agreed.

We actually moved from her watering hole to other bars and she was intent upon taking picture after picture of Ellie and me as we made our rounds. I knew that she had to be in excruciating pain but she was not backing down and she would not quit until we did.

When we arrived back at her home in Oakland she took her night time dose of morphine and went to bed. Ellie and I ate, got into our bed clothes and went outdoors and sat on the front porch of mom's modest home where we sat and drank, visited and smoked cigarettes until late into the night.

The following morning while having coffee our mom asked us what we had done the night before.

"Oh nothing really, we just sat on the front porch and visited." I said.

"You did what?" Our mother asked incredulously.

"We ate, put on our jammies and sat on the front porch to visit. We didn't go any where" I responded.

"You can't do that here!" she shouted in her limited capacity. "You can get mugged, raped or murdered here. You can not sit out doors at night."

Ellie and I just looked at one another feeling a bit perplexed. We were small town country girls and we had never even entertained the thought that there was any danger in sitting out doors after dark.

We assured our mother that we would not do it again.

The visit was briefly interrupted by a telephone call from Glenna who called to tell me that Roger had called her and asked that she take him to the hospital because he felt that another seizure was going to occur. He was alone and he knew that if he had a seizure again that no one would be there to call for help, so in my absence he called Glenna.

"He just kept asking for you." Glenna said.

I later spoke to Roger and he told me that he had smelled the scent that always preempted a seizure and he had felt confused so he'd had Glenna take him to the hospital.

It turned out to be a false alarm probably induced by the anxiety of my absence. I had always been there for him and this time I was not.

During this visit my mother attempted to give me her wedding rings.

"When I am gone they will be yours any way so take them now." She had said to me.

"Mom, I am not taking your rings." I had flatly stated. "Those rings were given to you by the only man that has ever made you happy and you will wear them to the end. I'll get them, don't worry about it."

There was no way that I could take the symbol of their love and have her face the end without them. They were obnoxiously large and not really pretty but the two stones were a full carat apiece and very valuable. Mom conceded to keeping her rings.

She actually liked the cologne that I wore better than the cologne that I had given her for Mothers Day. I shared this with Roger who had given me the cologne and he told me to give it to her. She wasn't willing to keep my cologne either.

As the visit was drawing to a close, I observed a book that Ellie was reading and I wanted to borrow it for the flight back to Florida. Ellie said that she was not done with it and that I could not take it.

Like a small child throwing a fit I went to my mother and said, "Mom, Ellie won't let me have her book!" I said.

My mother looked at me and without hesitation she said, "You can have it."

I was teasing of course but it was a precious moment and I laughed, "I can have it?"

"Yes," she said as she flexed her maternal authority, "you can have it."

I went to Ellie and said, "Mom said that you have to give me your book!"

We were joking around but the obvious point was that I was still getting my way even though I was now thirty six years old.

When I said my final good-bye to my mother we both knew that we would not see one another again in this life. I gave her a hug and we stared into one another eyes for what seemed like an eternity. There are no words for the sadness and fear that was looking back at me. I gave her one final hug and turned to catch my flight. I did not look back as the tears streamed down my cheeks.
When I boarded the plane my high end Calvin Klein cologne remained in my mother's bathroom, she still had her rings and I had Ellie's book for my flight back to Florida.

In addition to fighting throat cancer for ten years, our mother was also riddled with Rheumatoid arthritis and her feet and hands were gnarled and bent from surgeries in an effort to alleviate the crippling effects of the decease. In the final days of her life I received a very distressing phone call when she called to tell me that the rings that I had refused to take were now stolen. The loss of the rings was bad enough but the worst part was that the thief had beaten her to get them.

Due to the arthritis and the debilitating effects of it, she could not open her kitchen window if she shut and locked it so she left it ajar slightly so that she was able to open it.
Not a brilliant thing for her to do knowing that she lived in such a rough neighborhood and living alone, but she did it none the less.
She had noticed that when she went to the bank and got out five, six, eight hundred dollars at a time that it would turn up missing from her purse where she had left it. She confided to her best friend that she thought she was putting it somewhere and could not remember where she had put it due to the morphine. Her girlfriend later told us that she would come over and they would search the house but could never find the missing money. Eventually our mother got tired of misplacing her money so she did not withdraw any more. The first time that she did not withdraw any money from the bank she awoke to a predator in her bedroom. The morphine had worn off and she awoke to a black man standing in her bedroom and going through her personal belongings. She flew out of her bed and attempted to

attack the intruder and fought with him the entire length of her home. She lost the conflict obviously overcome by a healthy young man. She suffered contusions and bleeding, but her greatest loss was the wedding rings. When he broke an entry this time and found no money, he looked for something else of value and he found it. He took the rings.

It was a heartbreaking tragedy. I don't know if I was more upset that he got the rings or that he had beat the hell out a ninety pound woman that was dying of cancer. I only know that I was distraught and Roger was ready to fly our there and wait for the little bastard to show back up so he could shoot him. Of course he did not fly out there.

It was not long after that incident that my mother became gnarly when I phoned her to see how she was doing. The pain and the suffering were unbearable now and she really resented the intrusion when she was making an effort to survive another day. Speaking had become unbearable for her now and she did not want to have to speak on the telephone. I stopped calling her.

Then in October of 1995, our phone rang. I was sitting on the lanai to our apartment when Roger brought me the phone. I did not even have to ask who was calling because I knew. It was over and she was gone.

Ellie and I each flew back to Oakland to settle our mother's estate and to attend her services. Our mother had taken care of everything. Her cremation was already arranged and paid for, the burial at sea was already arranged and paid for, and we had nothing to do except to attend the services, go through her personal belongings and clear up the mess that was caused by her identity theft.

When Ellie and I entered our mother's home we sat down at her kitchen table a moment to develop a plan and the first thing that I said to Ellie was, "If there is one thing in this house that is worth us fighting over then you can have it, because there is no way that she had anything more important than you are to me."

Ellie agreed and we had no problem with the division of our mother's property. Boyd was expressly excluded from receiving any benefit upon her death and we both knew this.

Ellie also knew of a secret drawer beside her bed that our mother had told her about so we opened the secret compartment and found some old jewelry that we assumed was costume jewelry. Our mother had no idea what the stuff in the drawer was. The investigation turned up a lot of things that we had not expected though and eventually we had a post card collection from the turn of the century, the oldest bible that I had ever seen, black and white photos from WWII, a negative of General Macarthur as well as a matching photograph, a bookies horse race ledger from the nineteen twenties, and most importantly were pictures of Boyd and his family as she had monitored his life. She must have obtained the photographs from one of her brothers who forwarded them to her after had they received them. He had denounced her but she had maintained a small shrine for him despite his exclusion from her estate.

While Ellie and I were going through our mother's home we found eight unopened bottles of pure liquid morphine. We called Hope Hospice repeatedly and ask that they please come pick it up. We knew that the street value of the morphine was enormous and we also knew that we could be killed for it if the wrong people knew of its existence. We spent nearly a week with the stuff in the house before a Hope Hospice representative finally arrived to pick it up. She explained to us that it could not be re-administered to another patient because it had already been delivered to our mother.
"We don't care what you do with it," Ellie said, "just get it out of here. Give it to someone that needs it, but we don't want it here!"
The Hope Hospice representative took the morphine and Ellie and I relaxed a little bit after that.

Our mother's best friend told Ellie and me how the end had come for her and it was horrid. The doctors had told mom that eventually her jugular would burst externally and she would bleed to death within twenty four hours. As the doctors had predicted her jugular burst externally and there was blood everywhere, but she did not die within twenty four hours. In fact she did not die within forty eight hours, and after bleeding to death for two solid days and not dying she finally hooked her feeding tube up to two full bottles of liquid morphine and ended it herself. After setting herself up to die with lethal doses of morphine she informed her friend that when she slipped into a coma then her friend should call the ambulance and have her transported to the hospital and that is where she finally died.

The day of her services, we all congregated at her favorite 'watering hole' as she referred to it and we all had a drink in her memory before heading to Fisherman's Wharf in San Francisco. We were allowed a party of eight to attend for the sprinkling of her ashes off the coast of San Francisco Bay and all eight of us were congregated at the bar. After toasting her memory we then departed as a group and crossed the street to our vehicles. No one was crying but the tension was running high especially with Ellie and me. As we attempted to cross the busy street a motorist nearly ran over us and the driver laid on the horn.
Ellie responded first shouting, "Up yours!"
I am considerably more crass than Ellie and I followed suit with, "Fuck you!" as I saluted the driver with my middle finger.
One of our mother's male friends in attendance came up between us and grabbed each of us by the arm and quickly escorted us rather forcibly through the intersection and said to us in a commanding voice, "They will shoot you here!" He was obviously rattled and relieved that the motorist had actually allowed us to survive the incident. We continued toward the cars as he looked back over his shoulder.

The drive over the bridge was solemn as we drove to the peer. When we arrived Ellie and I marveled over the world famous sea lions that congregate at the peer and then we were on the boat that our mother had prepaid and prearranged for her own burial at sea. We rode on the boat for what seemed an eternity. In the salon there were snacks and coffee, but I preferred to ride on the stern of the vessel. The yacht made its way past Alcatraz on this lovely October day and the brisk wind blew through my hair as we cruised toward the sight where the short service would be said and our mother's remains would be sprinkled at sea.

Ellie and I had not come equipped with cold weather attire so we each were wearing faux furs that had belonged to our mother. One of those in attendance said to us when she saw us, "Oh this will be wonderful, one of the animal activists are likely to throw blood on us." She was dead serious but this fortunately did not occur. Apparently anything is possible in this region of the world. Motorists shoot one another and animal activists throw blood on people wearing fake furs. This was not a nice place to live. All of my fantasies of what a wonderful life it would be if I could just get here were all dashed by these harsh realities.

Eventually the vessel carrying our small group of mourners reached it's destination. A short service was said and then it was time to sprinkle her remains. I had thought that the Preacher or the Captain would do this but everyone looked for Ellie or me to do it. Neither Ellie nor I could empty the contents of the urn. "I'll sprinkle my buddy's remains," her best friend said. She grabbed the urn and dumped the contents into the crystal clear water of the bay. To my astonishment the ashes that were the remains of my biological mother literally glistened in the water as the sun shined down on them. It was my prayer on that day that the shimmering remains were a sign from heaven that she had finally found peace.

Ellie and I spent our remaining days at the house going through our mother's belongings and then in the evening went to mom's 'watering hole' and had drinks. A Patsy Cline song was playing on the juke box and I asked Ellie if mom had listened to her a lot before we had left for Illinois.

"She listened to her non stop." Ellie said.

That explained the warm comforting feeling that I got when I heard the song. It was a subconscious reaction to something that had made me feel safe as a small child.

I also asked Ellie who the old lady was that had given me Big Betsy McCall when I was a very small child.

Ellie grinned at me and hesitated to respond then she said to me. "She wasn't given to you; she was given to me by Grandma Judy."

"Then how did I come to think that she had been given to me?" I asked in utter confusion.

Ellie grinned again and said, "Because you threw such a fit when she didn't give you one that I gave her to you."

My mouth fell open in disbelief!. I had taken Ellie's doll from her! I had always gotten my way! What else had I robbed from my sister? I had even taken her book only a few months before.

Ellie was complacent about the exchange of the doll but I was not! I had packed her around with me as a comfort tool for more years than I could remember. She was currently perched on top of a pillow in my bedroom at home and she had not been my gift at all.

I felt terrible but Ellie was alright with it. The doll that had not really been given to me had been manufactured the year that Ellie was born. I was not given life for ten years after both of their existence had come to be.

Big Betsy McCall: manufactured in 1948 with her lovely white dress and shoes is now yellowed and tattered and she sits bare foot on top of my china cabinet. Her hair is covered with dust but she is still lovely in my eyes. She was a survival tool for a troubled child and together we have endured; although both of us are now showing signs of age.

Chapter 24

Ellie and I returned to our home in Illinois and Florida each of us carrying checks in the amount of twenty thousand dollars. We had selected what each of us wanted from our mother's estate without conflict and I had much of it shipped to my home. Ellie had taken our mother's Cadillac and she had packed the trunk and interior of the car to its maximum potential. She then drove from Oakland, California to her home in central Illinois. Since I had lost the rings that were to have been mine Ellie said that I could take all of the 'costume jewelry' that we had discovered in the secret drawer. In addition to bringing home the post card collection and the other trinkets from WWI and WWII eras I also brought home the 'costume jewelry' and had my grandmothers ornate furniture shipped to Florida.

When I arrived in Florida, I had some small insignificant diamonds removed from Lions Club pendants and had post earrings made from them. When I contacted a jeweler who was a dear friend and client I also gave him a very tarnished bracelet as well as an old wedding ring. I told the jeweler that I wanted him to repair the wedding ring so that I could wear it as a pinky ring and asked him to verify that the stones in the bracelet were real. If they turned up real I would probably piece it out for something else.

When the jeweler returned with my 'costume jewelry' he informed that the wedding ring was not repairable because the gold was too weak to hold new stones. The ring was very old, probably close to a hundred years old he had advised me. Then came the shocking good news, the bracelet that had four rubies and three diamonds were in fact real stones, each stone was cut with the Star of David and the bracelet had been hand crafted probably before WWI. Both the ring and the bracelet had belonged to my mother's mother in law and were made in the early 1900's. The bracelet alone was valued at around seven thousand dollars. The jeweler in fear that I would piece out the stones had the bracelet polished to bring out the luster. When I saw the polished bracelet I knew that there was no way that I could ever piece it out. Nor could I actually wear it, so except for very special occasion it sits in a safe deposit box for me to pass on to one of my children. The bracelet has the name of my mother's mother in law engraved in the back of the soft fourteen carat gold and the clasp works very gingerly. I wear the wedding set on my little finger daily.

The 'costume jewelry' did not replace my mother's wedding rings but in a strange way were even more priceless to me. They were accidental treasures found.

I took the post card collection dating back to 1906 to a local collector and asked him what the value was for it was as a set. He looked entirely too long at the collection before he offered me two hundred dollars for the entire collection. That was enough to tell me that it was probably worth closer to a thousand dollars so I simply closed the binder and told the collector that I didn't need the money and left. The post card collection also belonged to my step grandmother and is also in the safe deposit box. The bible I learned is worthless despite the leather binding and gold leave pages because it is the oldest book in print and there are too many to be obtained. To my frustration it carries no copy right date so I have no idea how old it really is, but I know that it was printed prior to 1909 due to a dated book mark found in it.

My mother had not left me great wealth but a wonderful piece of history.

Eventually her home was sold and Ellie and I took a loss of about forty thousand dollars below the appraisal, because an offer was made and the taxes were coming due. We did not want to pay the outrageous property taxes in California, so we let it go just get out from under the expenses that it was incurring. There were other complications with respect to insurance and the dwelling being uninhabited. So we took our losses that were not losses at all and we each made another forty thousand each from the sale of her home.

Ellie wisely put her money into interest bearing accounts. I was not so wise.

I had originally put my money into CDs but was not long before the new general manager at the marina decided that it was time to make a change. He was a pompous self important sexually discriminating thief and I intimidated him. Roger and I as a team were too powerful and had far too much popularity and influence over the very high end customers that frequented the marina. They valued our opinions and advice when dealing with their over priced toys. Many of them actually became friends and socialized with us out side of the marina. One of them actually sent a limo after me to join their party at a water front bar and the first person I ran into when I arrived was the general manager of the marina. I was in control of the service department and Roger was in control of his side of the marina. Between us we basically ran the day to day functions of the entire facility, but it was a huge business and there were many other contributors to the daily operations. Between Roger and I though we had a pretty good idea of what was happening on sight and we carried a lot of influence with our customers.

The general manager was also stealing the marina blind and exchanging work for personal favors. He would have his personal buddies as well as his own boat rebuilt at the marina's expense in exchange for painting his home, landscaping, lawn maintenance or what ever repairs or upgrades he felt needed to be addressed at his personal residence.

He knew that I had entirely too much awareness of what was happening in my department and eventually I would grow weary of giving my departments work away, so he had to do something to eliminate me. He was even more threatened by mine and Roger's relationship with one another and the customers that we worked with each day.

So one day in February a company meeting was held. In this meeting the pompous arrogant pig announced that one of the technicians was being promoted to service manager. I was dumbfounded.

He hadn't demoted me he had promoted a mechanic, which inadvertently had actually demoted me. I would probably have ridden out the storm despite the insult but I knew the mechanic too well and I knew that he possessed the same customer service skills as the two that had been my predecessors that had been let go seven years earlier. My power had just been jerked out from under me and I knew that I would become a full time janitor cleaning up behind the new service manager endlessly and I was not prepared to do that. I liked the mechanic very much personally and considered him a friend, but I felt that he was not equipped for the position that he had just been given.

Roger approached me at the door of my office and he said, "Well, I guess you're not long for this place huh?"

I just looked at him and rolled my eyes.

I was sitting on the money that my mother had left me and I had a very bad attitude about the mechanics promotion. I slept on it and the following day I walked into the general manager's office and told him to take this job and stuff it.

It was a stupid thing for me to do, because I had just done exactly what he wanted me to do, but I had been doing things my way far too long to just accept the change. I knew that I would become the under paid clean up lady and the promoted tech was going to make all the money.

I went home and attempted to start my own business in direct competition with marina.

I failed bitterly.

The effect of my mothers death probably had a greater impact on me psychologically than I actually realized, my divorce from the marina with all my co-workers that had become my extended family was devastating and then when my phone did not ring as I had anticipated when starting my business, I became very depressed and even more irresponsible. I went to the gym every morning where I worked out on weight lifting equipment and then after my workout, I went straight to a quaint little restaurant to drink beer at ten o'clock in the morning each day where I spent most of the remainder of my day. Most of the money that I had spent on the occupational license, the incorporation of my business, the printing, advertisement and mailings were all wasted money. The money that I spent on drinking was even more wasted money and it wasn't long before I was broke. The only intelligent thing that I did with my inheritance was to buy a reliable vehicle. To this day I still drive my tired old Honda Accord.

I was forced to go back to work and I did not find a satisfactory job for a very long time. I worked as a dispatcher for am appliance repair company for a while which I hated. While working as a dispatcher I was contacted and offered a job by a yacht brokerage. At least the brokerage job got me back on the water and near boats again but it wasn't the same. Yacht brokerage can be the most intense of occupations but when it is not intense it is also the most boring occupation on the planet. It was not a greatly rewarding profession but it paid the bills so I stuck it out.

Chapter 25

After seven years of living together and doing most everything else together, I convinced Roger that we should get married. It was more of a pragmatic decision that a romantic one. We were both confident of our relationship and harbored no fears of infidelity, but I had no health insurance and we decided that we wanted to purchase a home. It only made sense that we should bind legally. I had already had pre-cancer cells removed from my cervix and I felt at the age of thirty nine it was very risky for me to not have medical coverage and the paper work would look a lot better on the loan process if we shared the same last name.

Over the years we learned that each our parents had been married on the same day in March. Even more ironic is that Roger and I were both hired at the marina on June sixth. Neither of these occurred in the same years but both occurred the same day. Since both of our parents were now gone, it seemed only appropriate that we should be married on their anniversary date. We threw the wedding together in about ten days and on March 3rd, 1997 we were joined in matrimony.

Roger had said for years that if he ever got married again he was wearing a pair of shorts and deck shoes. At first I found this idea to be a bit repugnant but in the end I turned lemons into lemonade. Since this was neither of our first marriages it was totally inappropriate that I should where the traditional white gown so I selected something colorless. I wore a sleeveless silver sequined floor length gown that was spit to the knee with a pair of silver pumps. Roger wore a white tuxedo coat with tails over a white tuxedo shirt, a silver comber bun, a silver bow tie and of course a pair of white shorts and deck shoes. We were dressed in full Florida style and we looked great if not amazingly striking. Our wedding attire could not have been any more of an expression of our personalities.

He had made arrangements for a limousine to pick me and our children up at the apartment and transport us to the location where the ceremony was to take place. The limo arrived at our front door and Gabrielle, Seth, Roger's son, Jesse, and Emily all rode with me in the limo to the waterfront property where we were to be married. The limo driver was also a personal friend of ours and he had taken care of stocking the limousine with provisions before his arrival. Emily who was now seven was the most impressed with the ride in the limousine and could not believe that it came with champaign, beer and even cola's for her and her siblings.

The ceremony opened with the playing of *"Here and Now" performed by Luther Vandross and Emily walked to the waters edge as she dropped rose petals from her basket. Emily was followed by Gabrielle and then I made my entrance. At the close of "Here and Now" the vows were exchanged. Following the exchange of the vows and the rings, the ceremony was concluded with *Lynyrd Skynrd's "Freebird" and the following word were read over the very lengthy instrumental portion of that legendary song.

Freebird to Freebird

Never before have I felt so as one with another person as I do with you I have spent half of a life time lonely, always once removed, never quite connected, quite accepted or loved for the person that I was born to be.

Never before have I found someone whose interest so readily became mine and who in turn became interested in those which are mine.
Never before have I found someone who could without threat accept my friends and acquaintances and whose friends I could genuinely say that I too enjoy

Never before could I relax and simply enjoy life with all of its ups and downs and know that when I inevitably screwed up that I was not in danger of losing love or acceptance.

Never before have I felt so loved yet unpretentious and unrestrained.

In essence I feel that I have been blessed in finally finding you and Freebird to Freebird I know that we soar high and freely side by side.

*6 *7

Through the Eyes of Betsy McCall

I had written that years before as a Christmas gift for Roger after he had informed me that he would not be tied down and it seemed appropriate that it should be read over the melody of that very song on the day that we were joined in matrimony. Roger had no idea that I had arranged for that to occur and when the song began to play he jerked his head in shock toward the music then attempted to fight back the tears that sprang into his eyes as the words were read over the melody. My version of "Freebird" remains in its original frame with two birds in flight behind the lettering and is still on display in our living room.

As the reading of those words was drawn to a close we were pronounced husband and wife and Roger was instructed to kiss his bride. As the tempo of the song picked up to the rock and roll version, so did the conclusion of the ceremony and hugs and kisses were exchanged, congratulations shared, the champaign opened and shared by all! Even the children were each given a glass of bubbly. The wedding party had consisted of Roger and me of course, Gabrielle who was then seventeen was my maid of honor, Roger's friend Bill was his best man, Bill's wife was the notary that had just married us and Emily had been my flower girl. As we approached the limousine Emily began to cry because she was now excluded from the ride to the water front restaurant and could not ride in the limo as she had previously arrived. A thoughtful mother would have said, "Oh come on you can ride with us."

But I had just gotten married and the thought did not occur to me to bend the rules. Instead I said to her, "If you don't stop crying I am going to throw a fit at your wedding when I can't ride in the limousine with you and your husband." That lack of sensitivity is my one and only regret I have for our wedding day; that I had excluded my flower girl from the ride in the limousine to the reception.

Our attending friends that had been in charge of the camcorder and the boom box convinced her that she should ride with them and she was eventually transported by them to the restaurant along with Jesse and Seth. When we all arrived at the restaurant the limousine driver was relieved from his duties. He reluctantly complied but Roger was adamant that he need not stay and take us to any further destinations or wait for us to leave these festivities in several hours. As a friend he had provided the limousine at no charge. So our friend and limousine driver left us and we all entered the reception area for the party to follow.

I had made arrangements for a table of food and the bar was open for what ever beverage was desired by our small cluster of family and friends. The tapping of the glasses and beer bottles with spoons was none stop and Roger and I kissed more that day than I think we had in the previous seven years. It was a wonderful celebration and a good time was had by everyone. The kids took turns running the camcorder and some of the footage became a bit dizzying but at that point in time it only added to the effects of our festivities. The bouquet was thrown, the garter removed and thrown, our gifts were opened and the bottles and glasses continued to tingle by the spoons being tapped.

At the close of the celebration Emily sprinkled her remaining rose petals into the water.
"Those are for grandma where ever she is." I said to Emily as she sprinkled her petals into the Caloosahatchee River. On this day I had observed the old superstition that it is unlucky to get married without something old, something new, something borrowed something blue, and the something old was the ruby and diamond bracelet that had belonged to my step grandmother in law some seventy years before.

I had prepaid for the table of cold meats, cheeses, assorted breads, crackers and fruits but when I went to pay the bar bill before our departure, there was none. Bill and his wife had paid that monstrous expense. What a wedding gift!

In our Florida style wedding attire Roger and I went to our bar that we so often frequented and drank with more friends. I expected that we would just go home from the bar since we had already spent a small fortune but then Roger shocked me with the announcement that what we were going to Ft. Myers Beach to get a motel room. So off to the beach we went and found a vacancy water front motel room for two hundred dollars. We checked into the room and then went to a high end beach front restaurant for dinner. At the restaurant we were spotted by one of our neighbors and were presented with yet another bottle of champaign. Following our dinner and consuming another bottle of champaign we finally retired to our motel room.

Back in the motel room we consummated our marriage on the outside balcony overlooking the Gulf of Mexico. We were totally intoxicated and suddenly I realized that we were not alone. On the balcony beside ours was a cluster of people.
"Oh my God Roger, there are people over there!" I whispered to him.
"Screw them." He whispered back to me as we giggled through our inappropriate conduct.

The following morning Roger woke me at around six o'clock and said, "Get up, we've got this room until noon and we're going to get everything we can out of that two hundred dollars.
"I have nothing to wear except my gown." I said.
"I know, we'll go home and a get a change of clothes for you and get back before the traffic backs up on the bridge." He responded.
My head felt like it was the size of a watermelon but I complied.

We ran home and quickly returned to the beach for our first day of marriage together.
When I sat on the beach that morning and I looked at my wedding rings, there were no thoughts or feelings of regret. We both agreed that our wedding day had been the happiest day of both of our lives. I was certain that I had found true love and happiness at long last.

And Big Betsy McCall saw it all.

Epilogue

Mack Hunsdorfer recently moved out of his senior parent's home at the age of forty seven, he is currently unemployed although he did only recently sell his own business. Jay who is now forty has no permanent address, no driver's license, no telephone, and he has no permanent job. Despite his instability he continues to stay in communication with Emily.
Boyd is happily married to his second wife, Ellie and Joe are still happily married after thirty eight years, and Uncle Howard has remarried to a lovely woman and they have been together for twenty five years.

Clarice, Danielle, Mitch, Royce and Donna all have married with families of their own and live throughout the United States.

Gabrielle is now a registered nurse after putting herself through college on scholarships and student loans. She has indicated to me that she too battles the temptation to eroticize her feelings. Seth is still searching for himself and works two jobs. He too has suffered and has had episodes of cutting himself due to pent up anger. Emily is now in full blown puberty and growing lovelier every day. Emily still struggles with severe anger management problems, but hers is another story for some time in the future. Perhaps she will write her own book someday.

Roger is still employed at the marina after nineteen years and we are doing well. We purchased our home three months after our marriage and now spend most of our time doing home and pool maintenance and yard work. He sold his drag bike shortly before we purchased the home and now he lives vicariously through young NASCAR drivers on weekends, while he sits pool side sharing beer and popcorn with our Shar Pei named Brutus.

I spend my days doing what ever is necessary to keep the household running while writing this book.

Roger and I have had our share of difficulties and health problems but remain desperately in love.

End Notes

*1) and *2) Ira Levin, The Stepford wives, New York, Random House, 1st Edition, Published 1972

*3) W. Hugh Missildine, Your inner child of the past, New York, Simon and Schuster, Published 1963

*4) Corporate author(s), Twentieth Century-Fox Film Corporation; CBS Fox video, Peyton Place, New York, NY;; CBS Fox Video, 1957,1991

*5 and *7) Lynyrd Skynyrd Feebird, AMC Records Inc., (Allen Collins/Ronnie Van Zant) Duchess Music Corp/Hustlers Inc.,(BMI)

*6) Luther Vandross, Here and Now, Terry Steele and Da'v-et (David L Elliot) Ollie Brown Sugar music/Triolle Interprises (ASCAP)

Special thanks to the following:

To my wonderful but somewhat impatient husband Roger, for allowing me to pursue this ambition while his income alone kept our family fed and our bills one step ahead of the creditors.

To Buddy Dow who is employed by AuthorHouse as the Author Services Representative. Buddy whom I have never had the pleasure of meeting has held my hand through countless emails, telephone calls, and constant communications while informing or advising me through out the publication process.

To my siblings 'Ellie and Boyd' who rescued me as well when they made their own escape from our horrible unsupervised young existence. Also for the steadfast companionship they provided me throughout my painful childhood.

To my Oncologists Dr. Thomas Tuefel and Dr. James Rubenstein whose combined expertise in cancer treatment gave me wellness and the ability to pursue this passion.

To my daughter 'Emily' who endured many mornings when I asked that she be quiet while I read through or reworked a portion of the book before she left for school.

To my family: 'Uncle Howard, Aunt Elise,' and their five children for sharing and providing the wonderful childhood I now reflect upon with fond memories and gratitude.

And finally to God who is last but certainly not least, for *His* many blessings and extending my time on this planet so that I was able to fulfill this life long dream.

C. R. Perk

About the Author

She was born Charletta Raye Miller in a small oil drilling community in southern Illinois. At the age of five she was moved to central Illinois without the presence of her living mother.

She became a member of a large affluent family, but despite the many comforts of their home she longed for unity with her mother. Through her grief that seemingly no one understood, Charletta developed a survival technique of validating her feelings privately by hand writing them out on paper. Her story is one of courage, strength, heartbreak and constitution.

Charletta is now a cancer survivor, and has returned to her passion to write once more. She currently resides in Fort Myers, Florida with her husband and daughter.

CPSIA information can be obtained at www.ICGtesting.com
Printed in the USA
LVOW101719210312

274167LV00001B/260/A